Claudia Roden's
Invitation to
Mediterranean
Cooking

Claudia Roden's
Invitation to
Mediterranean Cooking

150 Vegetarian and Seafood Recipes

Claudia Roden

Photography by
Gus Filgate

MACMILLAN

For my children, Simon, Nadia and Anna, and for
Ros and Clive who have joined the family – with my thanks
for eating through the book with me.

First published 1997 by Pavilion Books Ltd

This edition published 1998 by Macmillan
an imprint of Macmillan Publishers Limited
25 Eccleston Place, London SW1W 9NF
and Basingstoke

Associated companies throughout the world

ISBN 0 333 62804 7

135798642

A CIP catalogue record for this book is available
from the British Library.

Designer: Janet James
Home Economist for photography: Maxine Clarke
Stylist: Penny Markham
Colour reproduction: D P Graphics, England
Printed and bound in Italy by New Interlitho

CONTENTS

INTRODUCTION

THE MEDITERRANEAN DIET – A MODEL OF HEALTHY EATING

In the late 1960s the world became aware of the work of the American nutritionist Ancel Keys, who studied the link between diet and disease of men in seven countries and found that almost all the countries around the Mediterranean had a lower rate of cardiovascular diseases, cancer and various other chronic diseases. His discoveries triggered a flood of research in all corners of the world. Some countries, such as Italy and Finland, changed the diet of whole villages and noted the results. Immigrant communities whose eating habits changed in new homelands were also studied.

Although there are many contradictions and confusion in nutritional theories, the results of these studies showed that despite other factors, such as genetics, lifestyle and environment, diet remained the obvious major cause of disease. The so-called Western diseases of affluence were linked to a diet low in fibre, high in sugar and saturated animal fats; and the diet of the Mediterranean countries – rich in grains, vegetables, fruit and nuts, with plenty of fish and little meat, and oil as the main cooking fat – came out as the ideal healthy diet.

A worldwide consensus gradually emerged about what to eat. The World Health Organization, the Food and Agricultural Organization and all the major world health reports have come up with the same recommendations: eat more wheat, rice, beans, lentils, chick peas and nuts, lots of fresh vegetables and fruit, more fish, less red meat, and cook with oil rather than butter. Many governments have issued food guidelines based on these recommendations.

Recently, olive oil has been heralded as an effective weapon in the fight against disease. Since time immemorial, it has been believed to have curative and nutritive properties – a panacea for all kinds of illnesses – and modern science has confirmed its beneficial qualities. It is high in monounsaturated fats and fatty acids and rich in vitamin E, which is an antioxidant that is believed to help prevent heart and lung diseases and cancer. Like all vegetable and seed oils, it is cholesterol-free. And it has the added effect of reducing so-called 'bad' cholesterol (low-density lipoproteins) and increasing 'good' cholesterol (high-density lipoproteins).

Of course, other parts of the world where people use large quantities of oil, vegetables, fruits and pulses could have been used as a model for healthy eating, but the Mediterranean style has been adopted as the best way to encourage people to change their eating habits because of its very special appeal. Mediterranean food is full of flavour, aroma and colour;

and it is familiar enough for us to feel comfortable with on an everyday basis. The area was, after all, the cradle of Western civilization and it has always been the foremost tourist destination. Furthermore, this corner of the world is so immensely seductive, with its blue sea and sky, magical light and scented air, fairs and street markets and open-air terraces, and casual and leisurely good-humoured way of life, that it represents an art of living and eating that we would like to emulate.

A CULINARY RENAISSANCE

For years, in restaurants and hotels around the Mediterranean, local cooking has been overshadowed by French classic cuisine. When tourism was born at the end of the nineteenth century and high society discovered the Côte D'Azure, the luxury hotels and restaurants adopted the grand style of French gastronomy; this became the model to which the hospitality trade across the entire Mediterranean, and indeed the world, aspired.

In more recent times, the move from countryside to towns, the mass-production of food, the arrival of convenience and fast foods, and mass tourism have all contributed to the loss of traditional regional cooking. A French sociologist remarked cynically that *la cuisine du terroir* (the regional cooking of the land) exists only in cookery books. But it is not quite so. Nostalgia for a vanishing heritage and the fear of losing cultural identity, as well as a general change of tastes and values, have resulted in a revival of interest in regional rustic cuisines and in cottage industries, not only in France but in all the countries around the Mediterranean.

The top French chefs in Provence and the Côte D'Azure who went through their Nouvelle Cuisine rebellion against 'mummified Parisian classicism', have now turned to regional produce and styles for inspiration for their creations. In Italy, where *piatti tipici*, as they call local regional dishes, began to appear on restaurant menus little more than a decade ago, professional cooks say they want to update and revitalize the old dishes, not embalm them. They call the trend *il recupero* and *la riscoperta*. In every country around the Mediterranean, including Turkey, Egypt, Morocco and Tunisia, restaurants that had once been ashamed to offer anything but French and international classics are now proud to serve their own local dishes.

Another phenomenon is the way Mediterranean foods, especially the rustic, country and 'poor' foods, have become fashionable all over the world and are considered representative of 'modern' cooking. Star chefs in Britain and America are inspired by the produce and styles of the Mediterranean, and supermarkets stock all the necessary ingredients. It is especially gratifying to see how healthy eating and the pleasures of the table have converged.

In the beginning interest was focused on the cooking of southern Italy and Provence. More recently it has spread to all the varied cuisines of the area, and in particular to the more exotic ones of the eastern and southern Mediterranean.

MEDITERRANEAN CUISINE:
A MANY-SPLENDOURED THING

Although Mediterranean dishes are extraordinarily varied and there are many cooking styles in the sixteen or so countries around the little inland sea, there is a certain unity throughout the Mediterranean basin, which means that if you know one cuisine, you will be able to understand the others, and many of the dishes can be seen as variations on a theme. The unity has to do with the sharing of climate and produce, with the intense traffic and trading activity between all the port cities, and with an incestuous history.

Since ancient times, settlers, colonizers and empires spread across the entire area, introducing new produce, utensils and methods, and leaving their mark everywhere. The first wave of colonists – the Phoenecians, Greeks and Romans – established the trinity of wheat, olives and vines. The Arabs, who were the dominant force from the seventh century (they occupied part of Spain for 700 years and Sicily for 200), established new trading systems and spread the cultivation of foods such as rice, sugar cane, apricots and oranges

(bitter oranges and lemons were known to the Romans), pomegranates, dates, bananas, artichokes, spinach and aubergines (eggplants). Other important influences were the kingdom of Catalunya, which conquered Sicily, Sardinia and Naples and penetrated the south of France; and the crown of Aragon, which had possessions around the Mediterranean. The Normans and the Republic of Venice, which had colonies as far away as Alexandria, also introduced their cooking styles to the Mediterranean shores. One of the greatest unifying forces was the Ottoman empire, which lasted for 500 years until its collapse in the early twentieth century. It spread a style of cooking, drawn from its conquered territories, to all the countries in the empire.

Apart from empires and colonists, movements of populations contributed to an interchange of cooking styles: for instance, the Moors returning to North Africa after their expulsion from Spain; Tunisians moving to Palermo to build the cathedral; Sicilian peasants brought to Algeria by the French colonists to work the land. And travellers went to and fro: troubadours and jongleurs from southern France were seen in Italy and Catalonia; spice merchants and itinerant traders were seen everywhere. More recently, the French *Pieds Noirs*, resettling in the south of France, and immigrant workers from North Africa have had an enormous impact.

A unified culinary culture was woven from these intermeshed threads, which made the Mediterranean a world of its own and has meant that Andalusia, Provence and southern

Italy have more in common with their maritime neighbours than with the northern regions of their own countries. Throughout the Mediterranean, cooks use the same clay pots, the same wood-burning ovens, pestles and mortars, skewers and grills. You find similar dishes – vegetables cooked in olive oil and eaten cold, stuffed vegetables, thick vegetable omelettes, rice dishes, creamy puddings and almondy pastries, and the same tomato sauce, which is the signature of Mediterranean cuisine. The olive tree has a strong historical and cultural association with the Mediterranean, and the juice pressed from olives is the traditional cooking oil of the region; although not all the countries use it exclusively, it is certainly used liberally, as is lemon juice. Most recipes call for garlic, though not usually in very large amounts and always in a way that softens the flavour, and herbs and spices add a beguiling touch. Combine this with the visual appeal of ingredients like peppers, tomatoes, orange pumpkin and black olives, and you get something quite enchanting.

There are, of course, also many differences that distinguish one country's cuisine from another's. Where the French use cognac, Sicilians use Marsala, and Spaniards use sherry. Where Italians use pecorino (Romano) cheese or ricotta, the French use goats' cheese or Gruyère, and the Greeks and Turks use feta. While a fish soup in the French Midi is flavoured with orange peel and saffron, in Italy it is flavoured with white wine, peperoncino (chilli) and parsley, and in Tunisia with cumin, paprika, cayenne and coriander (cilantro) leaves. Parsley, coriander (cilantro) and mint are favourite herbs in the eastern Mediterranean, while basil and marjoram are favourites in the western part. A Western Mediterranean dish may use vanilla or grated orange zest in place of the eastern Mediterranean orange blossom or rose-water and cinnamon. Egyptians mix fried garlic with crushed coriander seeds, and Turks combine cinnamon with allspice.

From the wealth of dishes of the area, I have picked only personal favourites. My concern was not to cover all of the countries or to feature famous dishes, or include an example of every type of food. It was to offer fresh, light, delicious, casual food for every day that is quick and easy to cook, as well as some more elaborate, exuberant dishes that are ideal for entertaining and special occasions and are fun to serve. Although the dishes are naturally in line with the ideals of healthy eating, the *pleasures* of cooking and eating are the main focus of this book.

Although there are no meat dishes in the book, the aim is to appeal to meat-eaters who wish to vary and extend their diet as well as to vegetarians. Meat has never featured largely in Mediterranean cooking. It was very highly prized, but the peasantry could hardly ever afford it. In some countries it was eaten only once a week, and sometimes only on festive occasions. In Christian countries, the medieval Church forbad meat on Fridays and during Lent, so for almost a third of the year, fish and legumes took the place of meat. Fish was prepared in a simple way, but a great deal of inventiveness and ingenuity went into creating vegetable dishes. Luckily, the area was blessed with a propitious climate and soil, and provided a wide variety of vegetables, nuts and fruit. That is why the Mediterranean is an eden for vegetarians.

Tips from a Mediterranean Kitchen
Planning a Vegetarian Meal

The book has been organized in short chapters to make it easy to select a vegetarian menu. Each chapter, except Vegetable Side Dishes, Desserts and Basics, contains recipes for good main dishes. A light summer meal can consist of a salad or two served with good bread, accompanied, if you like, with cheese, while a simple winter meal can be soup with bread. A family meal may be one dish such as a pasta, risotto or bulgur pilaf, an egg dish, cheese bake, tart, flan or gratin, served with a salad and followed by fresh fruit.

For a small dinner party, have a soup or appetizer to start with, and cheese and a dessert to follow. There are dishes, such as vegetable couscous, that can be served as a one-dish meal. For a grander affair for many people, you may like to serve a variety of appetizers and a main dish, which can be made in advance and reheated if necessary.

The Mediterranean way is to end a meal with fresh fruit, but I have included many desserts because we in the Anglo-Saxon world are particularly fond of them. At dinner parties, especially, people look forward to a sweet dessert. Most of the desserts in this book are made with fruits that celebrate the produce of the Mediterranean.

Planning a Fish or Seafood Meal

A fish soup accompanied by toasted bread can be a meal in itself, followed by fruit or a dessert. Or you can plan around a seafood pasta, couscous or fish flan. The most common Mediterranean way is to grill (broil) or fry fish as simply as possible. A marinade or dressing is the usual embellishment, while sauces are provided as accompaniments. You can start the meal with a vegetable soup or appetizer or with seafood such as prawns (shrimp), scallops or mussels. Serve the fish with a salad or with one of the many vegetable, rice or bulgur side dishes featured in this book.

About the Ingredients

Bulgur (cracked wheat): Also called *pourgouri* in Cyprus and *burghul* in the Arab world, bulgur is wheat that has been boiled and dried, then ground to various degrees of fineness.

Couscous: Hard wheat that has been ground to various degrees of fineness, then moistened and coated with fine flour. It is cooked by steaming. The varieties available in this country are mass-produced and pre-cooked.

Flat-leafed parsley: The parsley of the Mediterranean region is the flat-leafed variety, which has a different flavour to our curly-leafed parsley. But curly-leafed parsley may be substituted, if flat-leafed parsley is unavailable.

Olives: Olives are a symbol of the Mediterranean. They all ripen from green and yellow, through red and violet, to purple and black. Cured and preserved black and green olives are served as appetizers and for breakfast, to accompany bread and cheese, and also go into many dishes. It is important to choose a good-tasting variety. Try sampling a few different types; every Mediterranean country produces some very good ones. The fleshy Greek Kalamata, the Spanish Manzanilla, the small black Taggiasca from Liguria, and large green Cerignola of Puglia in Italy are famous, as are the sweet black wrinkled olives of Provence and the tiny ones of Nice. Unfortunately, all the varieties that are sold pitted are invariably bad or tasteless, so for recipes that require pitted or chopped olives you will have to stone them yourself.

Olive Oil: With the extraordinary range of fine extra virgin olive oils available now from different countries, and the growing snobbery and mystique that surrounds this newly fashionable product, it is good to explore the qualities of the different oils for yourself. Like everything else in matters of taste, the best olive oil is the one you like best. And since one olive oil may be good in one context while a different one is good in another, it is worth experimenting.

Oils vary in colour, flavour and aroma depending on the type of tree, the soil in which it grows, whether it grows on a hill or the plain or by the sea, the weather, when and how the olives are harvested, how ripe they are, how quickly the oil is extracted and by what means. The old traditional method is to crush and grind the olives, pits and all, and let the oil rise gradually to the top of the extracted liquid. New methods of production now most commonly used, called 'continuous' methods, separate the liquid from the solid paste, then the oil from the rest of the juice by spinning the paste or liquid at high speed in a drum or centrifuge. The extra virgin oils produced from first cold-pressings by either of these methods are the finest, with the richest flavour and aroma. The bottled varieties can be varietal oils from a single type of olive, or blends. The blending of oils of two or more varieties of different origin with complementary characteristics is an art that usually entails mixing neutral oils with strong-tasting ones to produce a perfect balance. The oils produced by single estates are the most prestigious and expensive, but some of the extra virgin oils produced more cheaply by large commercial operators can be wonderful too. Unfortunately, many of these are lacking in the desirable qualities, and many of the super-expensive oils are hardly worth the expense.

Oils can be light and delicate, or assertive and strong, and their flavours and aromas simple or complex. Flavours range from sweet to pleasantly bitter, through fruity, nutty, spicy and peppery. They can be upfront, or experienced as an aftertaste. Fragrance may be fruity, floral, nutty or grassy, elusive or intense. As with wine, some harvests produce exceptional oil, some more ordinary oils. But blended oils are always the same, as blenders seek to achieve consistency by adjusting their mixes. Their styles reflect local tastes and traditions as well as the preferences – for lightness, for instance – of consumer countries newly converted to olive oil.

You cannot tell the style or quality of an oil by the colour, although a dark green is generally characteristic of a fruity, bitter, astringent oil produced from green olives that

have not reached maturity, and golden yellow oils made from sweet ripe black olives late in the season (all olives start green and ripen to black). However, it is not uncommon for green leaves to be crushed with the olives to colour the oil.

In general, the best oils of Provence are light, sweet and fragrant; the oils of Greece are slightly bitter, assertive and hearty; while Portuguese oils are rough and rustic. Spain produces a variety of fruity aromatic oils – Catalan oils have a delicious almondy quality while Andalusian oils have a warm, sweet fruity taste and heady perfume. Italy is famous for the strongly assertive, bitter quality of its Tuscan oils whose peppery aftertaste grates the back of the throat, but the lesser known light, sweet, fruity oils from Liguria, Umbria and the Abruzzi, and the rich, fruity, peppery ones of Apulia, are also very appealing. While all Mediterranean countries produce a certain amount of olive oil, Turkey and Tunisia, where every bit of the countryside is dotted with olive trees, are important producers whose oils are not easily available in Europe. They do not benefit from EC subsidies and cannot afford to promote themselves. Much of the Tunisian product goes to Italy and some to Spain and France to be blended and re-exported. Some of the Italian blends also use Greek and Spanish oils.

Different types of oil are suitable for different dishes. There are no fixed rules, and tastes vary. The best extra virgin oils should be used raw, as a dressing. I like a light, fresh, non-astringent fragrant oil to dress salads, fish and boiled vegetables, and to blend into delicate raw sauces; and a rich, fruity oil for gazpachos and herby green sauces, to dress pasta and drizzle over grilled (broiled) or fried vegetables, meat or fish. A drop of strong-tasting, bitter, fruity or spicy oil will enhance the taste of a creamy soup, a stew or a tomato sauce and makes a rich dressing for pasta. For deep frying, use oils labelled 'ordinary virgin olive oil', 'refined olive oil' or simply 'olive oil'. These are produced from second or subsequent pressings, which have then been processed and refined to remove their acidity, and are usually bland.

Some people like to flavour their oil with aromatics such as garlic cloves, chillies, sprigs of basil, rosemary or thyme, bay leaves or fennel seeds. These should be left in the oil for two weeks, then removed, as they may rot.

Harissa: A fiery hot chilli and garlic paste with spices from North Africa which can be bought from supermarkets and Middle Eastern stores. It is best bought in a tube rather than in a tin as you need only a little at a time. To make it yourself, see page 219.

Pepper: Black pepper, preferably freshly ground, is used throughout the book, unless otherwise stated.

Pomegranate syrup: This is the concentrated syrup or molasses of boiled-down sour pomegranate juice. It is available in Middle Eastern stores.

ABOUT DRINKS

The traditional spirit of the Mediterranean is flavoured with aniseed – in France it is pastis, distilled from grapes; in the Middle East it is arak, raki, ouzo or zibib; and in Morocco it is mahia, which is made from figs or dates. They are always served with appetizers. Beer and whisky are other warm weather drinks. In Muslim countries the usual refreshments are pressed lemon, fresh fruit juices, iced syrups and yoghurt beaten with iced water or soda.

In non-Muslim countries wine is always served with meals. It is a habit worth adopting. A simple and robust wine with character and quality, which can stand up to an amalgam of flavours, is what you need. Vinegar and lemon will turn a thin dry wine flat, and sweetness will make it acid, while spices and chillies will kill a great and complex wine. A young vigorous wine with rough fruit goes well with sour, sweet, spicy and savoury flavours. With a fruity dessert you can serve a sweet wine.

Strong black coffee – Turkish or espresso – is the perfect end to a Mediterranean meal.

ABOUT MEASURES

I have sometimes given numbers of vegetables as well as the weight, only as a rough guide. Bear in mind that sizes vary considerably from one greengrocer and supermarket to another, let alone from one country to another, (I have found, for instance, that in different stores between 5 to 8 'medium' tomatoes weighed 500g/1lb).

The baking dishes I have used are generally round clay ones, but square and rectangular ones will do just as well. The size given is the diameter. I have also used round cake tins.

Mediterranean cooks are not over-concerned with precise measures and prefer to judge by eye if a dish is the right size. They also rely on their taste for adjusting seasonings and aromatics. I would like to encourage you to do the same and trust your good sense, because that really never fails, even if you are dealing with a dish that is new to you.

SALADS AND APPETIZERS

Salads and cold vegetable dishes, served as appetizers with drinks, or as side dishes, are some of the most appealing features of Mediterranean eating. They enliven a meal with their traditionally strong flavourings (spices and aromatics are meant to sharpen the appetite) and exuberant colours, and bring variety and excitement to the table. One advantage is that they can be prepared in advance. You can also make a meal out of two or three appetizers accompanied with bread, and perhaps cheese and olives.

60G/2½ OZ/1 BUNCH ROCKET
(ARUGULA) LEAVES

3 MEDIUM TOMATOES, QUARTERED

3 TBSP LIGHT EXTRA VIRGIN
OLIVE OIL

JUICE OF ½ LEMON

SALT AND PEPPER

ABOUT 6 SPRING ONIONS
(SCALLIONS), SLICED

ROCKET (ARUGULA) AND TOMATO SALAD

This is an Egyptian salad.

SERVES 4

Cut the rocket (arugula) leaves into ribbons. Put them in a bowl with the tomato quarters and dress with the remaining ingredients.

A MIXTURE OF SALAD LEAVES
(ABOUT 200G/7 OZ), SUCH AS
GEM (SMALL ROMAINE) LETTUCE,
OAK LEAVES, CURLY CHICORY
(CURLY ENDIVE), CHICORY
(BELGIAN ENDIVE), WATERCRESS,
ROCKET (ARUGULA), LAMB'S
LETTUCE (CORN SALAD),
DANDELION AND PURSLANE

½ –¾ CUP MIXED CHOPPED FRESH
HERBS, SUCH AS CHERVIL, BASIL,
MARJORAM, CHIVES, MINT, PARSLEY
OR CORIANDER (CILANTRO)

VINAIGRETTE (SEE PAGE 218)

MIXED GREEN LEAF AND HERB SALAD

This type of salad became famous long ago as the Provençal *mesclun* and now all our supermarkets sell packs of mixed leaves inspired by it.

SERVES 4

Put the salad leaves in a wide shallow bowl and sprinkle on the herbs.

Just before serving, dress the salad lightly with the Vinaigrette.

VARIATIONS

Add fried garlic slices or garlic croutons made by rolling small cubes of bread in olive oil flavoured with a little crushed garlic, and toasting them.

Sprinkle with fresh walnut halves.

RIGHT *Mixed Green Leaf and Herb Salad*

2 BUNCHES (ABOUT 250G/9 OZ) PURSLANE

4 PLUM TOMATOES, QUARTERED

2 SMALL OR 1 LARGE CUCUMBER, PEELED AND CUT INTO THICK SLICES

4 SPRING ONIONS (SCALLIONS), SLICED

VINAIGRETTE (SEE PAGE 218)

100G/4 OZ FETA CHEESE, CUT INTO 2 CM/¾ IN CUBES (OPTIONAL)

8 BLACK OLIVES (OPTIONAL)

PURSLANE SALAD WITH TOMATO AND CUCUMBER

Purslane is one of the Mediterranean salad leaves that has yet to be discovered here. You can find the fleshy leaves occasionally, sold in bunches, in Greek and Middle Eastern stores. You can shred them or leave them whole for this salad, which makes a light meal.

SERVES 4

Pull the purslane leaves off the stems. Put them in a bowl with the rest of the vegetables and dress with the Vinaigrette.

Garnish, if you like, with feta cheese and olives.

1 CURLY ENDIVE OR BATAVIA OR 2 GEM (SMALL ROMAINE) LETTUCES, CUT INTO RIBBONS

JUICE OF ½ ORANGE

JUICE OF ½ LEMON

½ TBSP ORANGE BLOSSOM WATER

2 TBSP SESAME, HAZELNUT OR A LIGHT EXTRA VIRGIN OLIVE OIL

SALT

2 LARGE ORANGES (SWEET OR SOUR), PEELED AND SLICED

LETTUCE AND ORANGE SALAD

Oranges are used in a variety of salads in Morocco, where they use the delicately flavoured argan oil (from the rare argan tree) to dress them. You may like to try sesame or hazelnut oil.

SERVES 4

Dress the lettuce with a mixture of the orange and lemon juice, orange blossom water, oil and salt. Scatter in a wide serving dish.

Lay the orange slices on top.

CHOPPED CUCUMBER AND MINT SALAD

**This Middle Eastern cucumber
salad is delicately scented and refreshing.**

SERVES 4

1 LARGE CUCUMBER, PEELED AND GRATED OR CHOPPED IN THE FOOD PROCESSOR

3 TBSP EXTRA VIRGIN OLIVE OIL

2 TBSP LEMON JUICE OR 1 TBSP WHITE WINE VINEGAR

1 TBSP ORANGE BLOSSOM WATER, OR TO TASTE

SALT

1 TBSP DRIED CRUSHED MINT LEAVES

A FEW BLACK AND GREEN OLIVES, TO GARNISH (OPTIONAL)

Drain the cucumber. Just before serving, put it into a serving bowl and mix with the rest of the ingredients. Garnish, if you like, with the olives.

WHITE HARICOT (NAVY) BEAN SALAD

**This is the famous Turkish piaz.
It makes a snack or light meal.**

SERVES 4

2 x 400G/14 OZ TINS OF WHITE HARICOT (NAVY) BEANS OR CANNELLINI BEANS

5 TBSP EXTRA VIRGIN OLIVE OIL

2 TBSP WHITE WINE VINEGAR

SALT AND PEPPER

1 MEDIUM MILD ONION, FINELY CHOPPED

3 TBSP CHOPPED FLAT-LEAFED PARSLEY

10 BLACK OLIVES

2 FIRM BUT RIPE TOMATOES, CUT INTO WEDGES

2 HARD-BOILED EGGS, SIZE 1 (U.S. LARGE), CUT INTO WEDGES

Drain the tinned beans, dress with oil, vinegar, salt and pepper, and mix with the chopped onion and parsley.

Serve garnished with olives, tomatoes and hard-boiled eggs.

OVERLEAF *From left to right: Lettuce and Orange Salad (page 18); Courgette (Zucchini) Pureé (page 26)*

2 FENNEL BULBS

VINAIGRETTE
(SEE PAGE 218)

FENNEL SALAD

**The delicate anise flavour of fennel is particularly
pleasant when it is eaten raw.**

SERVES 4

Cut the fennel bulbs in slices lengthways. Arrange on a
serving plate and pour on the Vinaigrette.

*250G/9 OZ (ABOUT 2 LARGE)
CARROTS, CHOPPED OR GRATED IN
THE FOOD PROCESSOR*

*3 TBSP GROUNDNUT (PEANUT) OR
LIGHT VEGETABLE OIL*

1 GARLIC CLOVE, CRUSHED

1/2 TSP CINNAMON

SALT

2–3 TBSP LEMON JUICE

*150ML/5 FL OZ/2/3 CUP PLAIN OR
THICK, STRAINED GREEK YOGHURT*

MOROCCAN CARROT SALAD
WITH YOGHURT

**This surprisingly soft, creamy salad
will do well as an appetizer or side dish.**

SERVES 4

Sauté the carrots in the oil with the garlic over low
heat, stirring often, for about 10 minutes, until slightly
softened but not coloured. Add the cinnamon, salt and
lemon juice and cook for about 5 more minutes.

Serve the carrots cold on a flat plate with the
yoghurt poured on top.

RIGHT *Fennel Salad*

500G/1LB (ABOUT 4 LARGE) CARROTS

2 GARLIC CLOVES, CRUSHED

1–2 TBSP WHITE WINE VINEGAR

4 TBSP EXTRA VIRGIN OLIVE OIL

1/2 TSP GROUND CUMIN OR CARAWAY SEEDS

6 BLACK OR GREEN OLIVES

1 PRESERVED LEMON PEEL (SEE PAGE 219), CUT INTO SMALL PIECES (OPTIONAL)

SPICY CARROT PURÉE

Many North African appetizers are strongly flavoured, usually with cumin, which is meant to whet the appetite.

SERVES 4

Boil the carrots in water until soft. Drain and mash them with a fork.

Add the garlic, vinegar, oil and cumin or caraway seeds and mix well. Serve cold, garnished with olives and preserved lemon peel, if using.

250G/9 OZ (2 LARGE) CARROTS, CUT INTO 2 CM/3/4 IN SLICES

250G/9 OZ (1 LARGE) SWEET POTATOES, CUT INTO 2 CM/3/4 IN CUBES

4 TBSP SEEDLESS RAISINS OR SULTANAS (GOLDEN RAISINS)

1/2 TSP POWDERED GINGER

1/2 TSP CINNAMON

SALT AND PEPPER

3 TBSP EXTRA VIRGIN OLIVE OIL

1 TBSP HONEY

JUICE OF 1/2 LEMON

CARROT AND SWEET POTATO SALAD

North African appetizers can be fiery or, like this one, sweet and delicate.

SERVES 4

Put the carrots and sweet potatoes in a pan with just enough water to cover.

Stir in the rest of the ingredients and simmer, uncovered, to reduce the sauce, for about 15 minutes, or until the carrots and sweet potatoes are tender and the sauce is syrupy and thick. Serve cold.

200G/ 7 OZ/ 1 CUP LARGE BROWN
OR GREEN LENTILS, SOAKED FOR
1 HOUR

SALT

1 MEDIUM ONION, CHOPPED

5–6 TBSP EXTRA VIRGIN OLIVE OIL

1 TSP GROUND CORIANDER

300G/ 11OZ SPINACH

JUICE OF ¹/2 – 1 LEMON

PEPPER

VARIATIONS

Use frozen leaf spinach.
Defrost and add to the
fried onion. Sprinkle with
salt and cook, stirring, for
5 – 8 minutes.

Use chick peas or white
haricot (navy) beans
(tinned if you like) instead
of the lentils.

For a different lentil salad
with tomato and cheese,
mix the cooked lentils with
3 medium diced ripe
tomatoes and 100g/4oz
mashed feta cheese and
dress with Vinaigrette (see
page 218).

LENTIL AND
SPINACH SALAD

**Spinach is paired with every one of the
Mediterranean pulses – chick peas (garbanzo
beans), beans, split peas and lentils –
in soups, stews and salads. It is one of the
age-old combinations that works well.
This salad is an old Arab favourite, often
accompanied by yoghurt.**

SERVES 4

Drain the lentils and simmer in fresh water for 20
minutes or until tender, adding salt towards the end,
then drain.

In a large pan, fry the onion in 2 tbsp of the oil over
medium heat until soft. Stir in the ground coriander.

Wash the spinach and remove the stems only if they
are tough. Drain, press all the water out, and put into the
pan with the onion. Sprinkle lightly with salt, cover with
a lid, and let the leaves steam for a moment or two over
low heat until they crumple into a soft mass.

Add the drained lentils, lemon juice, some pepper,
and the remaining oil, and mix well. Serve cold.

500G/ 1 LB (ABOUT 3 LARGE) COURGETTES (ZUCCHINI)

1–2 GARLIC CLOVES, CRUSHED

JUICE OF 1/2 LEMON

3 TBSP EXTRA VIRGIN OLIVE OIL

1/2 TSP GROUND CUMIN OR CARAWAY SEEDS

SALT

PINCH OF CHILLI POWDER

100G/ 4 OZ FETA CHEESE, CRUMBLED WITH A FORK (OPTIONAL)

6 GREEN AND BLACK OLIVES (OPTIONAL)

COURGETTE (ZUCCHINI) PURÉE

In this Moroccan salad with its exotic flavours, the usually bland courgettes (zucchini) are unrecognizable.

SERVES 4

Boil the courgettes (zucchini) in water until soft. Drain and mash with a fork. Add the garlic, lemon juice, oil, cumin or caraway, salt, and chilli powder, and stir well.

Garnish with feta cheese and olives, if you like.

500G/ 1 LB (ABOUT 3 LARGE)
COURGETTES (ZUCCHINI), CUT INTO
SLICES LENGTHWAYS

OLIVE OR VEGETABLE OIL FOR
FRYING

SALT

400ML/ 14 FL OZ/ 1³/4 CUPS PLAIN
OR STRAINED GREEK YOGHURT, AT
ROOM TEMPERATURE

VARIATIONS

The yoghurt may be
flavoured with 1 crushed
garlic clove and 2 tsp dried
crushed mint. It should be
at room temperature, even
when the courgettes
(zucchini) are served hot.

Another traditional
accompaniment is a fresh
Tomato Sauce (see page
218).

Aubergine (eggplant)
slices, cut lengthways, can
be prepared in the same
way. These are usually
salted and left to degorge
their juices for 30 minutes
before frying, but this step
is not obligatory.

FRIED COURGETTE (ZUCCHINI) SLICES WITH YOGHURT

For this traditional Arab way of serving courgettes (zucchini), the vegetables may be grilled (broiled) rather than deep-fried.

SERVES 4

Deep-fry the courgettes (zucchini) in hot oil until they are lightly browned, turning them over once, then drain them on paper towels and sprinkle with salt.

Alternatively, grill (broil) them. Arrange the courgette (zucchini) slices on a tray. Brush both sides very lightly with olive oil and sprinkle with salt. Put the tray under the grill (broiler) and cook the slices, turning them over once, until browned.

Serve hot or cold with yoghurt poured over.

500G/ 1 LB BABY AUBERGINES (EGGPLANTS)

SALT

5 GARLIC CLOVES, PEELED

4 TBSP EXTRA VIRGIN OLIVE OIL

2 TBSP POMEGRANATE SYRUP (ALSO SOLD AS MOLASSES OR CONCENTRATE)

JUICE OF 1/2 LEMON

1/4 TSP CHILLI PEPPER

1/2 TSP CUMIN

3 TBSP CHOPPED FLAT-LEAFED PARSLEY

MARINATED BABY AUBERGINES (EGGPLANTS)

You find baby aubergines (eggplants), which are about 10cm/4in long, in Indian and Middle Eastern stores. The dish keeps well for several days.

SERVES 4–6

Wash the baby aubergines (eggplants), remove the caps but leave the stems. Cut in half lengthways, not right to the end, so that the halves remain attached at the stem end.

Boil in salted water with the garlic cloves for 15 minutes, then drain.

For the marinade, mash the boiled garlic cloves and mix with the rest of the ingredients. Roll the drained aubergines (eggplants) in the marinade, opening them so that the cut sides can absorb it well. Leave for at least half a day and serve cold.

ABOUT *500G/ 1 LB (1 LARGE)*
AUBERGINE (EGGPLANT)

2 TBSP POMEGRANATE SYRUP
(ALSO SOLD AS MOLASSES OR
CONCENTRATE)

3 TBSP EXTRA VIRGIN OLIVE OIL

SALT AND PEPPER

1–2 CLOVES GARLIC, CRUSHED
(OPTIONAL)

2 TBSP CHOPPED FLAT-LEAFED
PARSLEY

MASHED AUBERGINE (EGGPLANT) WITH POMEGRANATE SYRUP

This is a Syrian version of the famous aubergine (eggplant) 'caviare' (see variation) which is found all over the Mediterranean. The dark, almost black, pomegranate syrup gives it an exciting sweet-and-sour flavour and intriguing colour (the syrup is sold in Middle Eastern stores as pomegranate concentrate or molasses). Accompany with warm bread for dipping.

SERVES 4

VARIATION

For the traditional aubergine (eggplant) 'caviare' add the juice of ½–1 lemon instead of the pomegranate syrup.

Roast and peel the aubergine (eggplant) as described on page 217. Press the juices out in a colander and chop the flesh finely with two pointed knives (this gives a better texture than blending in a food processor). Do the chopping in the colander, letting the juices escape.

Put the chopped aubergine in a bowl, add the rest of the ingredients and mix well. Spread the purée on a serving dish, sprinkle with parsley, and serve.

2 MEDIUM AUBERGINES
(EGGPLANTS), CUT INTO SLICES
ABOUT 1 CM/ 1/3 IN THICK

SALT

OLIVE OR VEGETABLE OIL FOR
FRYING

2–3 TBSP POMEGRANATE SYRUP
(ALSO SOLD AS MOLASSES OR
CONCENTRATE)

3 TBSP WATER

3 GARLIC CLOVES, COARSELY
CHOPPED

3 TBSP CHOPPED FLAT-LEAFED
PARSLEY

VARIATIONS

You can omit the
pomegranate syrup and
instead serve the fried
aubergine (eggplant) slices
spread with a layer of
thick, strained yoghurt, or
tossed in Tomato Sauce
(see page 218).

FRIED AUBERGINE (EGGPLANT) SLICES WITH POMEGRANATE SYRUP

In all Mediterranean countries fried aubergines (eggplants) are common everyday fare. This Syrian version, dressed with pomegranate syrup, is particularly delicious.

SERVES 4

Sprinkle the aubergine (eggplant) slices generously with salt, and leave them for 30 minutes to degorge their juices. Then rinse and dry with paper towels.

Deep-fry in about 1.25cm/½ in of oil. It should be hot at first, then lower the heat a little, so that the slices do not brown too quickly before they are soft inside. Turn over once. Drain on paper towels and pat gently with more towels on top.

Arrange on a serving dish. Mix the pomegranate syrup with the water and place a little on each aubergine (eggplant) slice.

Fry the garlic very briefly over low heat in 4 tbsp of the frying oil in a small pan, until golden.

Serve cold sprinkled with fried garlic and parsley.

2 GARLIC CLOVES, FINELY CHOPPED

2 TBSP EXTRA VIRGIN OLIVE OIL

500G/1 LB (ABOUT 6 MEDIUM) RIPE TOMATOES, PEELED AND CHOPPED

1–2 TSP GRANULATED SUGAR

SALT

1/2 TSP PAPRIKA (OPTIONAL)

A GOOD PINCH OF CHILLI PEPPER (OPTIONAL)

3 RED AND YELLOW (BELL) PEPPERS

(BELL) PEPPER AND TOMATO APPETIZER

This North African appetizer, called *shoucouka*, can be sweet or peppery hot. Serve it with bread.

SERVES 4

Fry the garlic in the oil until golden, then add the tomatoes, sugar, salt, and the paprika and chilli if using. Cook very gently for 30 minutes or until the sauce is thick and jam-like (jelly-like).

Roast and peel the (bell) peppers (for instructions, see page 216). Collect the juices that escape and add them to the tomato sauce.

Cut the peeled peppers into small squares and mix with the tomato sauce. Serve cold.

1 MEDIUM ONION, CHOPPED

4 TBSP EXTRA VIRGIN OLIVE OIL

3 GARLIC CLOVES, CHOPPED

400G/14 OZ (ABOUT 10 SMALL) FROZEN ARTICHOKE HEARTS OR BOTTOMS, SLICED OR QUARTERED

200G/7 OZ SHELLED GREEN PEAS OR PETITS POIS

200G/7 OZ SHELLED BROAD (FAVA) BEANS

2 TBSP CHOPPED FRESH MINT

2 TBSP CHOPPED FRESH DILL

SALT AND PEPPER

JUICE OF 1/2 LEMON

2 TSP GRANULATED SUGAR

ABOUT 4 TBSP WATER

TIP

It is difficult in this country to find baby artichokes that you can eat whole and it is a big effort to trim the usual artichokes to obtain the hearts. I use frozen artichoke hearts or bottoms (tinned ones are not much good). You can now get podded broad (fava) beans and peas at a few supermarkets. At an Iranian store near my house where I get my frozen artichoke bottoms (from Egypt in packs of 400g/14oz) I recently also found very good frozen skinned broad (fava) beans.

BRAISED BROAD (FAVA) BEANS, PEAS AND ARTICHOKES

A combination of broad (fava) beans and artichokes is found in almost every Mediterranean country. In Sicily green peas are added too. There is something very pleasing about the partnership. This can be served as an appetizer or a side dish.

SERVES 4–6

Fry the onion in the oil until golden.

Add the garlic, artichokes, peas and beans, and sauté gently, stirring, for about 2 minutes.

Add the mint and dill, salt, pepper, lemon juice and sugar, and moisten with the water. Cook with the lid on for 10 minutes or until the vegetables are tender, adding a little water if necessary.

Serve hot or cold.

NOTE To prepare and use fresh artichoke hearts, see page 217.

500G/ 1 LB SHIITAKE MUSHROOMS
OR A MIXTURE OF OTHER VARIETIES

1 MEDIUM ONION, CHOPPED

3 TBSP EXTRA VIRGIN OLIVE OIL

3 GARLIC CLOVES, CHOPPED

JUICE OF 1/2 LEMON

150ML/ 5 FL OZ/ 2/3 CUP FRUITY
DRY WHITE WINE

SALT AND PEPPER

3 TBSP CHOPPED FLAT-LEAFED
PARSLEY

MUSHROOMS WITH GARLIC AND WHITE WINE

This is a traditional way of cooking mushrooms in France and Italy. A mixture of wild mushrooms including boletus, chanterelles and morels makes a splendid but very expensive dish. Shiitakes are a very good alternative. Serve them, if you like, with toasted brioche halves or slices.

SERVES 4

Clean the mushrooms and cut very large ones into 2.5cm/1in pieces.

Sauté the onion lightly in the oil until soft. Add the mushrooms and garlic and cook until almost all their juices have evaporated. Add the lemon juice and the white wine, season with salt and pepper, and cook for a further 5–10 minutes.

Stir in the parsley and serve hot or cold.

1 LARGE ONION, CHOPPED

5 TBSP EXTRA VIRGIN OLIVE OIL

750G/ 1 1/2 LB SWEET POTATOES,
CUT INTO 4 CM/ 1 1/2 IN CUBES

1/2 –3/4 TSP GROUND (POWDERED)
GINGER

PINCH OF SAFFRON POWDER
(OPTIONAL)

1 TSP PAPRIKA

1 TSP CINNAMON

PINCH OF CAYENNE, TO TASTE

JUICE OF 1/2–1 LEMON

2 TSP GRANULATED SUGAR

SALT

4 TBSP CHOPPED CORIANDER
(CILANTRO) OR FLAT-LEAFED
PARSLEY

SWEET POTATO SALAD

In this Moroccan salad, the curious mix of sweet and spicy is quite delicious. It is nice as it is but you may add, if you like, a handful of black olives, chopped Preserved Lemon Peel (see page 219) and a tablespoon of capers.

SERVES 4

In a saucepan, fry the onion in 3 tbsp of the oil until soft. Add the sweet potatoes and just enough water to cover.

Stir in the ginger, saffron, if using, paprika, cinnamon, cayenne, lemon juice, sugar and salt. Cook, uncovered, for 15 minutes or until the sweet potatoes are tender, turning the potatoes over once; be careful not to let them overcook and fall apart.

The sauce should be much reduced to a thick, syrupy consistency. If it is not, transfer the potatoes with a slotted spoon to a serving dish and reduce the sauce further by boiling. Just before the end of cooking, stir in the coriander (cilantro) or parsley and the remaining oil. Serve cold.

750G/ 1 1/2 LB POTATOES

SALT

4 TBSP EXTRA VIRGIN OLIVE OIL

1 1/2 TBSP WHITE WINE VINEGAR

PEPPER

1/2 TSP HARISSA (SEE PAGE 219)
OR A GOOD PINCH OF CAYENNE
(OPTIONAL)

50G/2 OZ (1 SMALL TIN)
ANCHOVY FILLETS, FINELY
CHOPPED (OPTIONAL)

1–3 GARLIC CLOVES, CRUSHED
(OPTIONAL)

A GOOD BUNCH (ABOUT 1/2 CUP)
PARSLEY, FINELY CHOPPED

2 TBSP CAPERS, SQUEEZED TO GET
RID OF EXCESS VINEGAR

MASHED POTATO SALAD WITH ANCHOVIES

This Tunisian salad can be served as an appetizer or side salad and goes well with fish. The anchovies are optional.

SERVES 4–6

Peel and boil the potatoes in lightly salted water until soft, then drain, keeping a little of the cooking water.

Mash the potatoes with the oil and vinegar and 2–4 tbsp of the cooking water until they have a soft, moist texture. Add the rest of the ingredients and mix well. Serve cold.

150G/5 OZ/1 1/2 CUPS SHELLED
WALNUTS

1 1/2 –2 TBSP TOMATO PURÉE (PASTE)

1 SLICE WHOLEMEAL
(WHOLEWHEAT) BREAD, CRUSTS
REMOVED AND LIGHTLY TOASTED

8 TBSP EXTRA VIRGIN OLIVE OIL

2 TBSP POMEGRANATE SYRUP OR
THE JUICE OF 1/2 LEMON

1 TSP COARSELY GROUND HOT RED
CHILLI FLAKES OR A PINCH OF
CHILLI POWDER

1 TSP CUMIN

2 TSP GRANULATED SUGAR

SALT

SPICY WALNUT PASTE

This delicious Turkish relish, called *muhammara*, can be served as a dip with bread or to accompany a salad. It keeps very well for several days, so you can make a large batch. Pomegranate syrup, sold also as concentrate or molasses, is easy to find in Middle Eastern and sometimes Indian stores.

SERVES 6–8

Blend everything together to a paste in the food processor.

RIGHT *Spicy Walnut Paste and Focaccia (page 221)*

150G/ 5 OZ/ 3/4 CUP FINE OR
MEDIUM GROUND BULGUR

500G/ 1 LB (ABOUT 6 MEDIUM)
TOMATOES, PEELED AND PURÉED IN
A FOOD PROCESSOR

JUICE OF 1/2 LEMON

1 TSP TOMATO PURÉE (PASTE)

3–4 TBSP EXTRA VIRGIN OLIVE OIL

SALT

A PINCH OR MORE CHILLI FLAKES
OR CHILLI POWDER, TO TASTE

1 SMALL MILD ONION OR 5 SPRING
ONIONS (SCALLIONS), FINELY
CHOPPED

100G/ 4 OZ/ 2/3 CUP WALNUTS OR
PISTACHIOS, OR A MIXTURE OF THE
TWO

250G/ 9 OZ/ 1 1/4 CUPS MEDIUM
COUSCOUS

1 GREEN OR RED (BELL) PEPPER,
DICED

3 MEDIUM TOMATOES, PEELED
AND DICED

10 SPRING ONIONS (SCALLIONS),
THINLY SLICED

SALT AND PEPPER

JUICE OF 1 LEMON, OR MORE,
TO TASTE

5–8 TBSP EXTRA VIRGIN OLIVE OIL

A FEW SPRIGS OF FRESH MINT,
SHREDDED

A LARGE BUNCH (1/2 CUP) FLAT-
LEAFED PARSLEY, CHOPPED

BULGUR SALAD
WITH WALNUTS

In this scrumptious and nutritious Turkish
salad, called *batrik*, bulgur is soaked in
the juice of fresh puréed tomatoes and is enriched
with walnuts, pistachios and onions.
It can be made mild or hot with chilli pepper.

SERVES 4–6

Mix the bulgur with the blended tomatoes, lemon juice
and tomato purée (paste), and leave for an hour or until
the grain has absorbed the juice and become tender. Add
oil, salt and chilli flakes or powder to taste. Just before
serving add the onion and walnuts or pistachios.

COUSCOUS SALAD

I have not come across a couscous salad
in North Africa, but France is awash
with what they call *taboulé* (the name of the
Lebanese bulgur, mint and parsley salad).

SERVES 4–6

Put the couscous in a bowl, add 300ml/10 fl oz/1 1/4 cups
cold water and mix well. Leave for at least 30 minutes.
When the grain is swollen and tender, mix in the rest of
the ingredients.

RIGHT *Bulgur Salad with Walnuts*

2 LARGE ONIONS

125ML/4 FL OZ/ 1/2 CUP LIGHT EXTRA VIRGIN OLIVE OIL

150G/5 OZ/ 3/4 CUP LARGE BROWN LENTILS, SOAKED IN COLD WATER FOR 1 HOUR

700ML/ 1 1/4 PINTS/ 3 CUPS WATER

1/2 TSP CINNAMON

1/2 TSP ALLSPICE

150G/5 OZ/ 3/4 CUP AMERICAN LONG-GRAIN OR BASMATI RICE

SALT AND PLENTY OF PEPPER

VARIATION

Another method, which might be easier, is to boil the lentils and the rice in separate pans, then drain and mix together when each is done.

BROWN LENTILS AND RICE WITH CARAMELIZED ONIONS

In Syria and Lebanon this dish is called *mudardara*. In Egypt, it is known as *megadarra*. It is eaten cold or warm, usually accompanied by yoghurt and a cucumber and tomato salad. I have featured it before in my books but it is such a classic that it should be included here too. American long-grain rice does not need washing but basmati rice does. Pour boiling water over it, stir and leave for a few minutes, then rinse in cold water in a sieve.

SERVES 4–6

Prepare the garnish first. Slice 1½ onions into half moons and fry in 3 tbsp of the oil, over medium heat, stirring frequently, until they are very dark brown and almost caramelized. Set aside.

Chop the remaining onion and fry in 1 tbsp of the oil over medium heat until soft and golden.

Drain and simmer the lentils in the water with the cinnamon and allspice for about 15 minutes.

Add the rice and a pinch of salt and simmer, covered, for 18 minutes or until the rice is just tender.

Mix the lentils and rice with the fried onion and the remaining oil. Season with salt and pepper.

Serve warm or cold with the caramelized onions sprinkled on top.

2 LARGE CARROTS, CUT INTO
2 CM/ 3/4 IN SLICES

450G/ 1 LB/ 1 MEDIUM CELERIAC,
PEELED AND CUT INTO 2 CM/ 3/4 IN
CUBES

250G/ 9 OZ/ 1 MEDIUM SWEET
POTATO, PEELED AND CUT INTO
2 CM/ 3/4 IN CUBES

6 TBSP LIGHT EXTRA VIRGIN
OLIVE OIL

JUICE OF 1/2 LEMON

SALT AND PEPPER

1–2 TSP GRANULATED SUGAR

2 TBSP CHOPPED FRESH DILL

ROOT VEGETABLES
IN OLIVE OIL

**Vegetables cooked together in a mixture
of olive oil and water with herbs, and served
cold, are a speciality of the Eastern
Mediterranean. This winter selection has a
wonderful taste and texture.**

SERVES 4–6

Put the vegetables in a large pan with the oil and sauté over low heat, turning them occasionally, for 5 minutes.

Add the lemon juice, salt, pepper and sugar to taste and just enough water to cover. Simmer for 25–30 minutes or until the vegetables are very tender. Cover and cook for 20 minutes, then uncover and simmer to reduce the sauce.

Add the dill towards the end. Serve cold.

SOUPS

Soups are always a pleasant way to start a meal but, accompanied with a good slice of bread, a soup can also be served as a main course, or as a meal in itself. In the Mediterranean soups range from light vegetable creams and iced summer soups to aromatic broths with vegetables and rice, and rich and substantial winter combinations with lentils, beans and chick peas.

1.5KG/3 LB/1–2 MELONS,
TO YIELD ABOUT 1 KG/2 LB FLESH

2.5 CM/1 IN PIECE OF GINGER,
GRATED (OR USE ITS JUICE,
SQUEEZED OUT USING A GARLIC
PRESS)

1½–2 TBSP WHITE WINE VINEGAR,
OR TO TASTE

2 TBSP EXTRA VIRGIN OLIVE OIL

SALT AND WHITE PEPPER

6 TBSP GROUND ALMONDS

CHILLED MELON SOUP

**This delicately flavoured, refreshing
summer soup is thickened in the traditional
Mediterranean way, with ground
almonds. Choose sweet ripe melons.**

SERVES 4

Cut away the peel and rind and remove the seeds of
the melon or melons.

In a blender or food processor, liquidize the
flesh with the rest of the ingredients, then chill in
the refrigerator. The soup will thicken to a creamy
consistency when the almonds absorb the juice.

Serve cold.

1 RED (BELL) PEPPER, CUT INTO
PIECES

1–3 GARLIC CLOVES, CRUSHED

3 SLICES OF WHITE BREAD, CRUSTS
REMOVED AND CUT INTO PIECES

1.5KG/ 3¼ LB RIPE PLUM
TOMATOES, PEELED

6 TBSP SHERRY OR WHITE WINE
VINEGAR

5 TBSP EXTRA VIRGIN OLIVE OIL

SALT AND PEPPER

1–2 TSP GRANULATED SUGAR, OR
TO TASTE

FOR THE GARNISH

12 ICE CUBES

1 MEDIUM CUCUMBER, PEELED AND
FINELY DICED

1 RED ONION OR 4 SPRING ONIONS
(SCALLIONS), CHOPPED

1 GREEN (BELL) PEPPER, FINELY
DICED

RED GAZPACHO

There are many versions of the famous Andalusian cold soup. This thick, bright red tomato version, with no added water and a generous garnish, is my favourite. It is quite the best thing you could want to eat on a hot summer's day.

SERVES 6 OR MORE

Purée the (bell) pepper in a food processor. Add the rest of the soup ingredients and blend to a light smooth cream, adding a little cold water, if necessary, to thin it. Chill, covered, in the refrigerator.

Serve, adding 2 ice cubes to each soup bowl, accompanied by the garnish ingredients, each on a separate little plate.

2 LITRES/ 3½ PINTS/ 9 CUPS
VEGETABLE STOCK (BOUILLON)
MADE WITH 2½ CUBES

2–3 MEDIUM LEEKS, CUT INTO
2 CM/ ¾ IN SLICES

1 MEDIUM HEAD OF CELERY WITH
LEAVES, CUT INTO 2 CM/ ¾ IN
SLICES

1 LARGE POTATO, PEELED AND
DICED

SALT AND WHITE PEPPER

3 LARGE GARLIC CLOVES, CHOPPED

JUICE OF 1–3 LEMONS, TO TASTE

1 TSP GRANULATED SUGAR, OR
MORE TO TASTE

3 MEDIUM COURGETTES
(ZUCCHINI), CUT INTO 1.25 CM/
½ IN SLICES

6 ARTICHOKE HEARTS (FOR
PREPARATION, SEE PAGE 217), CUT
IN HALF – YOU MAY USE FROZEN
ONES (OPTIONAL)

100G/ 4 OZ/ ½ CUP PINE NUTS
OR BLANCHED ALMONDS, GROUND
IN A FOOD PROCESSOR

2 TBSP DRIED MINT

200G/ 7 OZ/ 1 CUP AMERICAN
LONG-GRAIN RICE, COOKED
(WEIGHT UNCOOKED)

GREEN VEGETABLE SOUP WITH LEMON

This is one of my favourite soups that our family had in Egypt. It is very lemony (its name, *hamud*, means lemony in Arabic) and also minty. We made it with chicken stock, but vegetable stock made with stock (bouillon) cubes will do. Cooked rice is added at the end, which makes it a substantial dish. Add the lemon to taste; you might not like it too sharp.

SERVES 6–8

In a large pan bring the stock to the boil. Add the leeks, celery and potato. Add salt, pepper, garlic, lemon juice and sugar and simmer for about 30 minutes.

Add the courgettes (zucchini) and artichokes, if using, and simmer for another 15 minutes. Add the ground pine nuts or almonds (the pine nuts give a particularly fine flavour), and mint, and cook for another 5–10 minutes. It is important at this point to taste and adjust the flavourings.

Serve in soup bowls over the hot rice.

A 750G/1½ LB PIECE OF ORANGE
PUMPKIN (WEIGHED WITH THE
SEEDS AND FIBRES REMOVED)

500G/1 LB (ABOUT 2 LARGE)
POTATOES, PEELED AND CUBED

1.25 LITRES/2 PINTS/5 CUPS MILK

SALT AND WHITE PEPPER

1 TBSP GRANULATED SUGAR,
OR TO TASTE

2 BAY LEAVES

1 SPRIG OF THYME

2 CINNAMON STICKS

150ML/5 FL OZ/⅔ CUP CRÈME
FRAÎCHE, SOUR CREAM OR THICK,
STRAINED YOGHURT

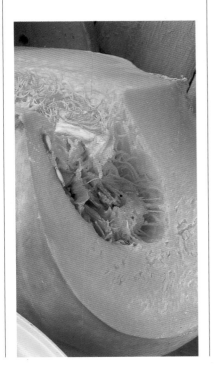

PUMPKIN SOUP WITH MILK

**There are pumpkin soups in every
country around the Mediterranean. This lovely
one is from Provence. You can usually get
orange-fleshed pumpkins in Indian and Middle
Eastern stores throughout the year.
Because the taste of pumpkin varies, it is
important to get the right balance of
salt and sugar. Start with a little of each, then
taste, and add more if necessary.**

SERVES 4

Peel the pumpkin and cut the pulp into cubes. Put it in a pan with the potatoes and milk, a little salt, pepper and sugar, the bay leaves, thyme and cinnamon sticks.

Simmer, covered, on low heat, for 20–25 minutes or until the potatoes and pumpkin are very soft.

Remove the bay leaves, thyme and cinnamon sticks and mash the vegetables with a potato masher. Adjust the seasoning and add water to thin the soup, if necessary. Cook for a further 1 or 2 minutes.

Serve hot, garnished with a dollop of crème fraîche, sour cream or yoghurt, or let people help themselves.

500G/ 1 LB (ABOUT 2 LARGE)
POTATOES

1.5 LITRES/ 2¹/2 PINTS/ 6¹/4 CUPS
WATER OR VEGETABLE STOCK
(YOU MAY USE A STOCK
(BOUILLON) CUBE)

250ML/ 8 FL OZ/ 1 CUP FRUITY DRY
WHITE WINE (OPTIONAL)

250G/ 9 OZ SHIITAKE MUSHROOMS

2 GARLIC CLOVES, CRUSHED

4 TBSP LIGHT VEGETABLE OIL

SALT AND PEPPER

A LARGE BUNCH (ABOUT ³/4 CUP)
FLAT-LEAFED PARSLEY, FINELY
CHOPPED

1 LEMON, CUT INTO WEDGES

150ML/ 5 FL OZ/ ²/3 CUP CRÈME
FRAÎCHE (OPTIONAL)

MUSHROOM SOUP

**This soup, thickened with potato rather than flour,
has a wonderful fresh taste.**

SERVES 4

Peel the potatoes and cut them into pieces. Put them in a pan with the water or stock and the wine, if using, and simmer until the potatoes are soft. Then crush them with a potato masher.

Chop the mushrooms in a food processor. In a frying pan, sauté the mushrooms and garlic in the oil for 5 minutes, stirring constantly. Pour into the pan with the crushed potatoes.

Add salt and pepper and simmer for a few minutes. Just before serving, add the parsley and heat through. Serve accompanied with lemon wedges and, if you like, crème fraîche.

*350G/12 OZ SPINACH OR
FROZEN LEAF SPINACH*

1 MEDIUM ONION, CHOPPED

*3 SPRING ONIONS (SCALLIONS),
FINELY CHOPPED*

*2 TBSP SUNFLOWER OR
VEGETABLE OIL*

*100G/4 OZ/1/2 CUP AMERICAN
LONG-GRAIN RICE*

*750ML/1 1/4 PINTS/3 1/2 CUPS
WATER*

1/4 TSP TURMERIC (OPTIONAL)

SALT AND WHITE PEPPER

*500ML/18 FL OZ/2 1/4 CUPS
YOGHURT*

1 GARLIC CLOVE, CRUSHED

SPINACH AND YOGHURT SOUP

**You find many different yoghurt
soups in the Eastern Mediterranean.
This hot version is exquisite.**

SERVES 4

Wash the spinach and remove the stems only if they are thick and hard. Defrost if using frozen spinach. Drain and cut into strips.

In a large saucepan, fry the onion and spring onions (scallions) in the oil until soft.

Add the rice and stir to coat it with oil. Pour in the water, add the turmeric, if using, season with salt and pepper and simmer for 15 minutes.

Add the spinach and cook for 5 minutes or until it softens and the rice is tender. The rice should not be too soft and mushy.

Beat the yoghurt with the garlic, then beat it into the soup. Heat through but do not boil or the yoghurt will curdle. Serve at once.

1 MEDIUM ONION, CHOPPED

1 SMALL CARROT, FINELY CHOPPED

A BUNCH OF CELERY LEAVES
(¹/₂ CUP), CHOPPED

4 TBSP SUNFLOWER OR VEGETABLE
OIL

200G/7 OZ/1 CUP SPLIT RED
LENTILS

1 LITRE/1³/₄ PINTS/4¹/₂ CUPS
VEGETABLE STOCK (YOU MAY USE
1 STOCK (BOUILLON) CUBE)

SALT AND PEPPER

³/₄–1 TSP CUMIN

JUICE OF ¹/₂ LEMON

1 LARGE ONION, CUT IN HALF
THEN SLICED

VARIATION

Before serving, stir in 4
chopped garlic cloves fried
in 2 tbsp olive oil with
1 tsp ground coriander and
2 tsp dried crushed mint.
A pinch of chilli pepper
may be added too.

RED LENTIL SOUP

**There are several versions of this
popular Middle Eastern soup. The flavouring
here is rather delicate, but you can
make it more spicy following the variation.**

SERVES 4

Soften the chopped onion, carrot and celery leaves in
2 tbsp of the oil in a large saucepan.

Add the lentils, stock, salt and pepper and simmer
for 30–45 minutes, until the lentils have disintegrated.
Add water if the soup needs thinning and stir in the
cumin and lemon juice.

Meanwhile, fry the sliced onion in the remaining
oil over medium-high heat, stirring often until crisp and
very brown – almost caramelized.

Serve the soup hot. Garnish each serving with a
scattering of fried onions.

125G/4½OZ/½ CUP PEARL
BARLEY

1.5 LITRES/2½ PINTS/7 CUPS
WATER, OR MORE

1 MEDIUM ONION, QUARTERED

1 MEDIUM CARROT, CUT INTO
THICK SLICES

1 CELERY STALK, CUT INTO THICK
SLICES

2 GARLIC CLOVES, PEELED

SALT AND PEPPER

400G/14 OZ TIN WHITE HARICOT
(NAVY) OR CANNELLINI BEANS

2 LEMONS, QUARTERED

EXTRA VIRGIN OLIVE OIL

CREAM OF BEAN AND BARLEY SOUP

This deliciously creamy and satisfying soup is from Italy.

SERVES 6

Put the barley in a pan with 1 litre/1¾ pints/4½ cups of the water. Bring to the boil and skim the surface.

Add the onion, carrot, celery and garlic and simmer for 1 hour or until the barley is very soft, adding more water if it becomes too dry. Season with salt and pepper to taste.

Pour the soup in batches into the food processor with the drained beans and enough water to obtain a creamy soup. Blend to a cream, adding more water if necessary. Return to the pan to heat through.

Serve hot with the quartered lemons and pass around a bottle of olive oil to drizzle into the soup.

250G/9 OZ/1½ CUPS CHICK PEAS
(GARBANZO BEANS), SOAKED IN
WATER FOR AT LEAST 1 HOUR OR
OVERNIGHT

3 LITRES/5½ PINTS/14 CUPS
WATER

1 LARGE ONION, COARSELY
CHOPPED

400G/14 OZ TIN CHOPPED
TOMATOES

3 CELERY STALKS AND LEAVES,
SLICED

2 TBSP TOMATO PURÉE (PASTE)

PEPPER

½–¾ TSP GROUND GINGER

1 TSP CINNAMON

200G/7 OZ/1 CUP LARGE BROWN
OR GREEN LENTILS, SOAKED FOR 1
HOUR, THEN DRAINED

SALT

JUICE OF ½ LEMON

500G/1 LB (ABOUT 4)
COURGETTES (ZUCCHINI), SLICED

100G/4 OZ VERMICELLI,
BROKEN INTO BITS BY CRUSHING
IN YOUR HANDS

A LARGE BUNCH (½ CUP) FLAT-
LEAFED PARSLEY, COARSELY
CHOPPED

A LARGE BUNCH (½ CUP)
CORIANDER (CILANTRO), COARSELY
CHOPPED

CHICK PEA (GARBANZO BEAN) AND LENTIL SOUP

This rich and filling winter soup is the Moroccan *harira*. It tastes just as good the day after it's made.

SERVES 8–10

Drain the chick peas (garbanzo beans) and put them in a large pan with the water, onion, tomatoes, celery, and tomato purée (paste). Add pepper and simmer, covered, for 1 hour or until the chick peas are very tender.

Add the ginger, cinnamon and lentils and cook for 20 minutes, or until the lentils are soft. Add salt to taste.

Add the lemon juice, courgettes (zucchini) and vermicelli, and more water if necessary, and cook for 10 more minutes. Just before serving, add the parsley and coriander (cilantro).

PIES AND TARTS

Pies and tarts are perfect buffet food and make ideal main dishes for dinner parties. The Eastern Mediterranean specializes in pies made with filo pastry, filled with cheese or spinach, or, more unusually, with mashed aubergine (eggplant) or pumpkin. The Western Mediterranean is justly renowned for its open vegetable tarts, some of the most delightful of which are to be found in the South of France.

1 RECIPE FILLING (CHOOSE ONE OF THOSE GIVEN ON PAGES 63–5)

4 SHEETS OF FILO

3 TBSP MELTED BUTTER OR VEGETABLE OIL

1 EGG YOLK, SIZE 1 (U.S. LARGE), MIXED WITH 1 TSP WATER

2–4 TBSP SESAME SEEDS TO SPRINKLE (OPTIONAL)

TIP

There may be problems with the frozen commercial filo. Too often the sheets are stuck together and tear when you try to separate them. A few brands are invariably good, so when you find a good one, keep to it. You can also get the fresh variety in Greek and Middle Eastern bakeries and groceries. If using frozen filo, defrost 3 hours before you are ready to use it.

FILO ROLLS

A filo pie accompanied by a salad makes an attractive meal. There are dozens of traditional pies made with filo, with different shapes, sizes and fillings, in all the countries that were once part of the Ottoman Empire. One of the easiest shapes to prepare is a roll that can be cut into portions at the table. Fill it with one of the fillings given on the following pages.

TO MAKE 2 FILO ROLLS TO SERVE 4

Pre-heat the oven to 180°C/350°F/Gas 4.

Prepare one of the fillings and be ready to work fast with the filo. Take out one sheet and lightly brush with melted butter or oil. Place another sheet on top and brush with melted butter or oil.

Spoon half the filling in a fat line along one long edge, about 2.5cm/1in from the edge and 4cm/1½in from the two ends. Lift the edge over the filling and very carefully roll up into a long thin roll, folding the ends in midway so that the filling does not ooze out. You must do this quickly because the filling is moist and if it lies too long on the filo, the pastry will be too wet to handle. Placing the sheets on a tea towel and lifting the towel makes it easier.

Brush the top of the roll with egg yolk and water mixture and, if you wish, sprinkle with sesame seeds. Repeat the whole process with the next two sheets of filo.

Bake for 45 minutes or until crisp and brown.

500G/ 1 LB FRESH OR FROZEN
WHOLE LEAF SPINACH

100G/ 3½ OZ COTTAGE CHEESE

100G/ 3½ OZ FETA CHEESE,
MASHED

2 EGGS, SIZE 1 (U.S. LARGE),
LIGHTLY BEATEN

SALT, IF NECESSARY, AND PEPPER

A GOOD PINCH OF NUTMEG

SPINACH FILLING

FILLS 2 ROLLS TO SERVE 4

Wash the fresh spinach, remove the stems only if they are tough, and drain.

Put the leaves in a large pan, cover, and cook over low heat for a few minutes only, until they crumple into a soft mass. Drain and press as much of the water out as you can. If using frozen spinach simply thaw and squeeze all the water out with your hands. If there is liquid, the pastry will become soggy and tear.

Combine the spinach with the rest of the filling ingredients. When adding salt, take into consideration the saltiness of the feta cheese.

500G/ 1 LB MUSHROOMS, SLICED

4 TBSP VEGETABLE OIL OR LIGHT
EXTRA VIRGIN OLIVE OIL

3 GARLIC CLOVES, CRUSHED

SALT AND PEPPER

4 TBSP FLAT-LEAFED PARSLEY,
CHOPPED

125G/ 4½ OZ RICOTTA

MUSHROOM FILLING

**This is an Italian filling used for cannelloni
but it also makes a good filling for a filo roll.**

FILLS 2 ROLLS TO SERVE 4

Sauté the mushrooms briefly in the oil with the garlic until tender, adding salt and pepper. Finish over high heat to reduce the juices. The mushrooms should be almost dry.

Add the parsley and allow to cool, then mix with the ricotta.

125G/ 4¹/₂ OZ EDAM, GRATED

125G/ 4¹/₂ OZ GOUDA, GRATED

125G/ 4¹/₂ OZ CHEDDAR, GRATED

125G/ 4¹/₂ OZ COTTAGE CHEESE

2 EGGS, SIZE 1 (U.S. LARGE), LIGHTLY BEATEN

PEPPER TO TASTE

VARIATIONS

Add 3 tbsp finely chopped dill or mint and ¹/₄ tsp nutmeg to the filling.

Alternative fillings are cottage cheese and feta, or these two with Gruyère.

750G/ 1¹/₂ LB AUBERGINES (EGGPLANTS)

125G/ 4¹/₂ OZ GRUYÈRE, GRATED

WHITE PEPPER

¹/₄ TSP NUTMEG (OPTIONAL)

2 EGGS, SIZE 1 (U.S. LARGE), LIGHTLY BEATEN

CHEESE FILLING

Filo rolls filled with this mild-tasting cheese mixture can be served as a main course or as a tea-time savoury.

FILLS 2 ROLLS TO SERVE 4–8

Put all the ingredients in a food processor and blend to a homogenous paste.

AUBERGINE (EGGPLANT) PURÉE FILLING

FILLS 2 ROLLS TO SERVE 4

Prick the aubergines (eggplants) with a knife in a few places and roast them in a 250°C/480°F/Gas 10 oven for 30 minutes, turning them once. Or put them under the grill (broiler) for 15–20 minutes and turn them until the flesh feels soft and the skin is blackened.

Peel in a colander and chop the flesh, letting the juices drain out. Then mash with a fork, still in the colander, and mix with the rest of the filling ingredients.

1 KG / 2 LB SLICE OF ORANGE
PUMPKIN, CUT INTO PIECES

125 ML / 4 FL OZ / 1/2 CUP WATER

100 G / 3 1/2 OZ / 1 CUP FRESHLY
GRATED PARMESAN CHEESE

2 TSP GRANULATED SUGAR

SALT TO TASTE

2 EGGS, SIZE 1 (U.S. LARGE),
LIGHTLY BEATEN

PUMPKIN FILLING

**You can find orange pumpkin in Indian
and Middle Eastern stores almost
throughout the year. It is sold in slices,
with the seeds and fibres removed.**

FILLS 2 ROLLS TO SERVE 4

Put the pumpkin in a pan with the water and steam, with the lid on, for 15–20 minutes, or until the pumpkin is very soft. Drain, return to the pan, and mash with a potato masher or a fork. Cook over a low heat to dry the paste out, stirring with a wooden spoon.

Mix with the rest of the ingredients. When adding salt, take into consideration the saltiness of the cheese.

150G/ 5 OZ FETA CHEESE

150G/ 5 OZ COTTAGE CHEESE

3 EGGS, SIZE 1 (U.S. LARGE)

3 TBSP CHOPPED FLAT-LEAFED
PARSLEY

125G/ 4½ OZ/ 5 SHEETS FILO

25G/ 1 OZ/ 2 TBSP UNSALTED
BUTTER, MELTED

300ML/ 10 FL OZ/ 1¼ CUPS MILK

CREAMY CHEESE BAKE
WITH FILO PASTRY

**In this version of the Turkish *sutlu borek*, filo pastry
is baked in a light creamy custard and becomes
soft, like sheets of ever-so-thin pasta. Accompanied
with a salad, it makes a scrumptious, homely meal.**

SERVES 4

Pre-heat the oven to 180°C/350°F/Gas 4.

To prepare the filling, mash the feta with a fork
and mix with the cottage cheese, 1 egg and the parsley.

Open out the sheets of filo, leaving them in a pile.
Brush the top one lightly with melted butter and fit it,
buttered side up, into a greased round baking dish about
30cm/12in in diameter, bringing the sheet up the sides
and folding it. Fit the second sheet over it and brush
lightly with butter.

Spread the filling evenly over the pastry. Cover
with the remaining sheets, brushing each with melted
butter and folding them. Fold the top one so that it
presents a smooth surface and brush with butter.

Bake for 15 minutes until lightly coloured, then
remove from the oven.

Lightly beat the remaining 2 eggs with the milk
and pour over the hot pie (you do not need to add salt
because the feta cheese is very salty). Return to the oven
and bake for about 30 minutes or until the custard is
absorbed and set and the top of the pastry is golden.

Serve hot, cut into wedges.

125G/4¹/₂ OZ/¹/₂ CUP UNSALTED BUTTER

250G/9 OZ/2 CUPS PLAIN (ALL-PURPOSE) FLOUR

¹/₄ TSP SALT

1 EGG, SIZE 1 (U.S. LARGE), LIGHTLY BEATEN

1–2 TBSP MILK (IF REQUIRED)

¹/₂ EGG WHITE, SIZE 1 (U.S. LARGE), TO GLAZE (OPTIONAL)

SAVOURY SHORTCRUST PASTRY (TART DOUGH)

This classic shortcrust pastry works well with all kinds of fillings.

ENOUGH FOR A 28CM/11IN TART TO SERVE 6

Pre-heat the oven to 180°C/350°F/Gas 4.

Cut the butter into small pieces and rub it into the flour and salt with your hands until it becomes like damp sand in texture.

Add the egg, mix well, and work very briefly with your hand until the dough holds together in a soft ball, adding a little milk if necessary. Cover in cling film (plastic wrap) and leave in a cool place for 1 hour.

Grease a 28cm/11in pie pan, a tart pan with a removable bottom, or flan mould, and line the bottom and sides with the dough by pressing it in with the palm of your hands (with this soft dough, it is easier to do this than to roll it out).

To bake blind (partially bake) the crust before putting in the filling, prick the bottom in a few places with a fork, brush with egg white and bake for 10–15 minutes. Remove from the oven and let it cool. Pour in the filling mixture and bake for 30 minutes or longer, depending on the filling.

1 RECIPE SAVOURY SHORTCRUST PASTRY (TART DOUGH) (SEE PAGE 67)

1 EGG WHITE, SIZE 1 (U.S. LARGE)

1 LARGE OR 2 SMALL FENNEL BULBS, QUARTERED AND SLICED

SALT

2 EGGS, SIZE 1 (U.S. LARGE), LIGHTLY BEATEN

125 ML / 4 FL OZ / 1/2 CUP DOUBLE (HEAVY) CREAM

125 ML / 4 FL OZ / 1/2 CUP MILK

100 G / 4 OZ GRUYÈRE, EMMENTAL OR FONTINA CHEESE, GRATED

PEPPER

PINCH OF NUTMEG

VARIATION

Instead of fennel, use 6–8 celery stalks.

CHEESE AND FENNEL TART

The combination of cheese with the delicate flavour of fennel makes a lovely filling.

SERVES 6–8

Pre-heat the oven to 200°C/400°F/Gas 6.

Prepare the pastry shell. Brush it with egg white, prick it all over with a fork, and bake it blind (partially bake) for 10 minutes. Let it cool.

Boil the fennel slices in salted water until they soften, then drain.

Beat the eggs with the cream and milk and mix in the cheese, pepper, a little salt (taking into account the saltiness of the cheese) and nutmeg.

Spread the drained fennel pieces over the bottom of the cooled pastry shell, and pour the cheese mixture on top.

Bake for 30 minutes and serve hot.

1 RECIPE SAVOURY SHORTCRUST PASTRY (TART DOUGH) (SEE PAGE 67)

1 EGG WHITE, SIZE 1 (U.S. LARGE)

500G/ 1 LB SHIITAKE MUSHROOMS

4 TBSP EXTRA VIRGIN OLIVE OIL

125ML/ 4 FL OZ/ 1/2 CUP FRUITY DRY WHITE WINE

SALT AND PEPPER

4 EGGS, SIZE 1 (U.S. LARGE), LIGHTLY BEATEN

200ML/ 7 FL OZ/ 1 SCANT CUP SINGLE (LIGHT) CREAM

PINCH OF NUTMEG

MUSHROOM TART

The mushrooms in this tart are given a delicate wine flavour. I use shiitake mushrooms, but you may use wild mushrooms such as ceps and morels if you prefer.

SERVES 6

Pre-heat the oven to 180°C/350°F/Gas 4.

Make the shortcrust pastry (tart dough) and leave in a cool place for about 1 hour, then roll out and line a 30cm/12in flan mould or pie pan, pressing it up the sides.

Brush the pastry top with egg white and bake it blind (partially bake) for 15 minutes. Let it cool.

For the filling (start when the dough is resting), wash and drain the mushrooms. Trim the root ends if necessary. Leave them whole or cut in half if too large. Heat the oil in a large pan over medium heat, add the mushrooms and sauté for 2 minutes, stirring and turning them over. Add the wine, salt and pepper and cook for about 10 minutes, until the mushrooms are tender, turning them over gently.

Beat the eggs with the cream and the strained juices from the mushrooms, which together with the reduced wine should amount to 200ml/7fl oz/1 scant cup. Add more salt and pepper to taste and a touch of nutmeg. Arrange the mushrooms in the cooled pastry case with their tops showing. Pour the flan mixture over them and bake for 45 minutes or until the cream has set.

Serve hot.

*250G/9 OZ BOUGHT PUFF PASTRY,
DEFROSTED*

1 EGG WHITE, SIZE 1 (U.S. LARGE)

1 LARGE ONION, FINELY CHOPPED

4 TBSP EXTRA VIRGIN OLIVE OIL

2 GARLIC CLOVES, FINELY CHOPPED

SALT AND PEPPER

*5 RIPE BUT FIRM PLUM TOMATOES,
CUT INTO 0.5CM/ 1/4 IN SLICES*

1/2–1 TSP GRANULATED SUGAR

12 BASIL LEAVES, SHREDDED

VARIATION

You may use 500g/1lb
cherry tomatoes cut in half
and arranged with the cut
sides up.

TOMATO TART

**This is a beautiful tart, exquisite and fresh
tasting, and very simple to make.**

SERVES 4

Pre-heat the oven to 230°C/450°F/Gas 8.

Roll out the puff pastry into a round to fit it into a
30cm/12in tart pan. (This pastry shrinks quite a bit and
will turn out much smaller when it is baked, even if you
let it hang over the sides.) Put it in the refrigerator for
30 minutes.

Brush the pastry case with half the egg white (this
prevents it from getting too soggy with juice), prick the
bottom all over with a fork (so that it puffs up evenly),
and bake it blind (partially bake it) in the hot oven for 10
minutes or until it puffs up and is golden. Take it out,
turn it over, brush the other side with the remaining egg
white and return it to the oven for another 8 minutes or
until this side is crisp and brown. Let it cool.

Fry the onion in 2 tbsp of the oil until soft. Add the
garlic and fry, stirring until golden. Remove from the
heat. Allow to cool then spread a layer all over the baked
pastry case. Sprinkle very lightly with salt and pepper.

Arrange the tomato slices on top of the onions, so
that they overlap in circles. Brush with the remaining
olive oil and sprinkle lightly with salt, pepper and sugar.

Place the filled tart in the oven and bake for 15–20
minutes. Serve sprinkled with shredded basil leaves.

PASTA

A century and a half ago, the foods of Bologna — the pastas with meat sauces in particular — came to represent the ideal Italian cuisine. Pellegrino Artusi, the author of Italy's most famous cookery book, *La scienza in cucina e l'arte di mangiare bene* (Science in the Kitchen and the Art of Eating Well), published in 1891, told his readers to 'take a bow when you meet Bolognese cooking'. Even in the fifties and sixties Bolognese cooks were still winning all the prizes, but these days it is the vegetable and seafood pastas of southern Italy and Sicily that are fashionable.

500G/1 LB SHIITAKE MUSHROOMS,
OR A MIXTURE OF WILD
MUSHROOMS

1 MEDIUM ONION, CHOPPED

3 TBSP EXTRA VIRGIN OLIVE OIL

1 GARLIC CLOVE, FINELY CHOPPED

JUICE OF 1/2 LEMON

150ML/5 FL OZ/2/3 CUP DRY
WHITE WINE

A FEW SPRIGS OF MARJORAM,
CHOPPED

SALT AND PEPPER

250ML/8 FL OZ/1 CUP DOUBLE
(HEAVY) CREAM

400G/14 OZ TAGLIATELLE OR
TAGLIERINI

1 MEDIUM ONION, CHOPPED

4 TBSP OLIVE OIL

1/2 GEM (SMALL ROMAINE)
LETTUCE, SHREDDED

125ML/4 FL OZ/1/2 CUP VEGETABLE
STOCK OR WHITE WINE

500G/1 LB FRESH SHELLED OR
FROZEN PETITS POIS, DEFROSTED

500G/1LB FRESH SHELLED OR
FROZEN BROAD BEANS, DEFROSTED

2 TSP DRIED CRUSHED MINT

SALT AND PEPPER

4 FROZEN ARTICHOKE HEARTS OR
BOTTOMS, QUARTERED

400G/14 OZ PASTA

GRATED PARMESAN CHEESE

PASTA AND MUSHROOMS

**Wild mushrooms make this a royal dish but are costly.
Shiitake mushrooms are a good alternative.**

SERVES 4

Wash the mushrooms and trim the root ends if necessary. Cut very large ones into 2.5cm/1in pieces.

Sauté the onion lightly in the oil over medium heat. Add the mushrooms and garlic and cook until nearly dry. Add the lemon juice and white wine, marjoram, salt and pepper and cook for 2 minutes. Add the cream, and cook until the sauce is thick.

Cook the pasta in boiling salted water until *al dente*, drain and serve at once with the sauce spooned on top.

PASTA WITH PEAS, BROAD (FAVA) BEANS AND ARTICHOKES

SERVES 4

Fry the onion in 2 tbsp of the oil until soft. Add the gem (small romaine) lettuce and sauté until it wilts.

Add the stock or white wine, the peas and beans and the dried mint. Season with salt and pepper and simmer for a few minutes until the vegetables are just tender. Add the artichokes and heat through.

Cook the pasta in boiling salted water until *al dente*, drain and mix with the remaining oil. Serve with the sauce poured over, accompanied with Parmesan.

1 LARGE AUBERGINE (EGGPLANT), CUT INTO 2 CM/ ³/₄ IN CUBES

SALT

2 YELLOW AND RED (BELL) PEPPERS

OLIVE OIL

3 GARLIC CLOVES, PEELED AND CHOPPED

500G/ 1 LB (ABOUT 6 MEDIUM) TOMATOES, PEELED AND COARSELY CHOPPED

PEPPER

1 ¹/₂ TSP GRANULATED SUGAR

400G/ 14 OZ SPAGHETTI

8 BLACK OLIVES, PITTED AND CHOPPED

1 TBSP CAPERS, SQUEEZED OF THEIR VINEGAR

3 TBSP SHREDDED OR TORN BASIL LEAVES

GRATED PECORINO (ROMANO) OR PARMESAN CHEESE (OPTIONAL)

SPAGHETTI WITH (BELL) PEPPERS AND AUBERGINES (EGGPLANTS)

This Sicilian pasta is called *Vesuvio* because the colours resemble the lava boiling out of the volcano.

SERVES 4

Sprinkle the aubergine (eggplant) with salt and leave for 1 hour, then rinse and dry in a cloth.

Roast the peppers (for directions see page 216). When cool enough to handle, peel and de-seed them and cut them into ribbons.

Fry the aubergine (eggplant) cubes in hot oil briefly until tender and lightly browned, turning them over once, then drain on paper towels.

In a large pan, fry the garlic in 2 tbsp of oil until it begins to colour. Add the tomatoes, season with salt, pepper and sugar and simmer for 15 minutes.

Boil the spaghetti in plenty of salted water until *al dente*, then drain.

Just before you are ready to serve, add the olives and capers, the aubergines (eggplants), (bell) peppers and the basil to the tomato sauce, and heat through. Pour over the pasta.

Serve with pecorino (Romano) or Parmesan cheese.

500G/ 1 LB FRESH SPINACH OR
FROZEN WHOLE LEAF SPINACH,
DEFROSTED

2 GARLIC CLOVES, CHOPPED OR
CRUSHED

2 TBSP SUNFLOWER OIL

SALT AND PEPPER

175ML/ 6 FL OZ/ ³⁄₄ CUP DOUBLE
(HEAVY) CREAM

3–4 TBSP PINE NUTS, RAW OR
TOASTED

400G/ 14 OZ GREEN LINGUINE

SALT

50G/ 2 OZ/ 4 TBSP BUTTER, CUT
INTO PIECES

GRATED PARMESAN OR PECORINO
(ROMANO) CHEESE

GREEN LINGUINE WITH SPINACH AND PINE NUTS

This is beautiful to look at and delightful to eat.

SERVES 4

Wash and drain the spinach. Remove the stems only if they are tough. If using frozen spinach, defrost.

In a very large pan over medium heat, sauté the garlic lightly in the oil until golden, then add the fresh spinach. Put the lid on and let the spinach cook by steaming in the water that clings to it, stirring occasionally. As soon as it crumples into a soft mass – it does so very quickly – remove from the heat. (Frozen spinach needs only a few minutes cooking.)

Season with salt and pepper, and stir in the cream and pine nuts.

Drop the linguine into plenty of vigorously boiling salted water and cook until *al dente*. Drain and serve mixed with the butter and topped with the spinach sauce.

Accompany with grated cheese.

750G/ 1 1/2 LB CHERRY TOMATOES,
CUT IN HALF

SALT

3–4 GARLIC CLOVES, CHOPPED

1–1 1/2 SMALL HOT RED CHILLI
PEPPERS, SEEDED AND CHOPPED
(OPTIONAL)

125 ML/ 4 FL OZ/ 1/2 CUP EXTRA
VIRGIN OLIVE OIL

4 SUN-DRIED TOMATOES, FINELY
SLICED (OPTIONAL)

A LARGE BUNCH (3/4 – 1 CUP)
MIXED FRESH HERBS, SUCH AS BASIL,
MARJORAM, OREGANO, MINT,
CHERVIL, CHIVES AND TARRAGON,
CHOPPED

400G/ 14 OZ SPAGHETTI OR
OTHER PASTA

GRATED PECORINO (ROMANO) OR
PARMESAN CHEESE

SPAGHETTI WITH HERBS AND ROASTED CHERRY TOMATOES

SERVES 4

Cook the tomatoes, cut side up, under the grill (broiler), until they soften slightly, and sprinkle very lightly with salt.

For the sauce, fry the garlic and chilli peppers in 2 tbsp of the oil until the aroma rises, then remove from the heat. Mix with the remaining olive oil, the sun-dried tomatoes, if using, and the herbs.

Cook the pasta in boiling salted water until *al dente* and drain. Mix with the sauce and serve topped with the grilled (broiled) cherry tomatoes.

Accompany with grated cheese.

GRAINS:
BULGUR, RICE AND COUSCOUS

Wheat, along with the olive tree and the grape vine, was part of the famous triad that the Greeks and Romans planted throughout the ancient world, and is eaten today in the forms of pasta, bulgur (cracked wheat) in the eastern Mediterranean and couscous in North Africa. But while bulgur is the staple food of the eastern Mediterranean countryside, in the cities it is rice, first introduced by the Arabs, that is the everyday fare.

350G/12 OZ AUBERGINES
(EGGPLANTS), CUT INTO
3 CM/1¼ IN CUBES

SALT

1½ LARGE ONIONS, SLICED

SUNFLOWER OR LIGHT VEGETABLE
OIL

350G/12 OZ/2 CUPS BULGUR,
PREFERABLY COARSELY GROUND

800ML/1¼ PINTS/3¼ CUPS
BOILING WATER OR VEGETABLE
STOCK (YOU MAY USE A STOCK
(BOUILLON) CUBE)

PEPPER

200–250G/7–9 OZ HALUMI
CHEESE, CUBED

BULGUR WITH CHEESE AND AUBERGINES (EGGPLANTS)

This Syrian dish, which combines bulgur with the chewy, salty *halumi* cheese and aubergines (eggplants), can be served as a main course.

SERVES 4–6

Sprinkle the aubergines (eggplants) generously with salt and leave in a colander for 1 hour to degorge their juices, then rinse and dry with paper towels.

Fry the onions in 2 tbsp of oil over medium heat until golden. Add the bulgur and boiling water or vegetable stock. Season with salt and pepper and stir well, then cook over very low heat, covered, for about 15 minutes or until the water has been absorbed and the bulgur is tender.

Fry the cubed aubergines (eggplants) briefly in hot oil, turning them so that they are tender and lightly coloured all over. Lift out and drain on paper towels.

Stir 5 tbsp of oil into the bulgur. Add the cheese and the aubergines (eggplants) and gently mix them in. Heat through, covered, until the cheese is soft.

Serve immediately.

1 MEDIUM ONION, CHOPPED

5 TBSP SUNFLOWER OR
VEGETABLE OIL

250G/ 9 OZ/ 1 1/2 CUPS BULGUR,
PREFERABLY COARSELY GROUND

4 MEDIUM TOMATOES, PEELED
AND CHOPPED

500ML/ 18 FL OZ/ 2 1/4 CUPS
VEGETABLE STOCK

SALT AND PEPPER

2 TBSP CHOPPED FRESH MINT

BULGUR PILAF WITH TOMATOES

Bulgur can be found coarsely ground in speciality stores. This can be served as an accompaniment to fish or mixed vegetable dishes, gratins or flans, egg dishes and cheese bakes.

SERVES 4

Fry the onion in 2 tbsp of the oil over medium heat until soft. Add the bulgur, tomatoes and stock, salt, pepper and mint. Stir well and cook, covered, for 15 minutes or until the liquid is absorbed and holes appear at the top. Add the remaining oil, then turn off the heat and leave to sit, covered, for 20 minutes. Serve hot.

500ML/ 18 FL OZ/ 2¼ CUPS
VEGETABLE STOCK

5 TBSP SUNFLOWER OR
VEGETABLE OIL

250G/ 9 OZ/ 1½ CUPS BULGUR,
PREFERABLY COARSELY GROUND

2 TBSP RAISINS

SALT AND PEPPER

3 TBSP PINE NUTS

BULGUR PILAF WITH
RAISINS AND PINE NUTS

**This is another side dish that can
be served with vegetarian flans and gratins,
egg and cheese dishes, and mixed
vegetables. It also goes well with fish dishes.**

SERVES 4

Bring the stock with 4 tbsp of oil to the boil. Add the bulgur and the raisins and a little salt and pepper (you may not need any salt as the stock is already salty).

Stir well and cook, covered, for 15 minutes, until the liquid is absorbed and holes appear at the top. Turn off the heat and leave to sit, covered, for 20 minutes.

Fry the pine nuts in 1 tbsp of oil over medium heat, shaking the pan, until they are lightly golden. Stir them into the bulgur and serve.

1 GARLIC CLOVE, FINELY CHOPPED

2 TBSP EXTRA VIRGIN OLIVE OIL

500G/ 1 LB (ABOUT 6 MEDIUM) TOMATOES, PEELED AND CHOPPED

ABOUT 175ML/ 6 FL OZ/ 3/4 CUP DRY WHITE WINE

SALT AND PEPPER

1–2 TSP GRANULATED SUGAR, TO TASTE

250G/ 9 OZ/ 1 1/4 CUPS ROUND RISOTTO RICE

TOMATO RISOTTO

There is a version of rice cooked with tomatoes in almost every country around the Mediterranean. This Provençal method uses wine to give a delicious flavour. It is a good accompaniment to vegetable flans and gratins, egg dishes, cheese bakes and mixed vegetables. It also makes a hearty first course.

SERVES 4

In a large pan over medium heat, fry the garlic in the oil over low heat until it begins to colour.

Add the tomatoes, wine, salt, pepper and sugar and simmer for 15 minutes.

Add the rice and cook, covered, over very low heat, for about 20 minutes. Add a little more wine if it becomes too dry.

Serve hot or cold.

500G/ 1 LB FRESH SPINACH

1 LARGE ONION, CHOPPED

4 TBSP LIGHT VEGETABLE OIL

300G/ 11 OZ/ 1½ CUPS RICE

500ML/ 18 FL OZ/ 2¼ CUPS VEGETABLE STOCK OR WATER

SALT AND PEPPER

1 TSP GRANULATED SUGAR

JUICE OF ½ LEMON, OR TO TASTE

VARIATION

Serve 280ml/½ pint/1¼ cups plain yoghurt as an accompaniment, flavoured, if desired, with one crushed garlic clove.

RICE WITH SPINACH

This beautiful Turkish pilaf is often accompanied by yoghurt. It can be served, like the other rice side dishes, to accompany most vegetable dishes and can also be a first course.

SERVES 4

Wash and drain the spinach and cut it coarsely or leave whole. Remove the stems only if they are tough.

Fry the onion in the oil in a large pan over medium heat until soft.

Add the rice and stir well, then add the stock or water, salt, pepper, sugar, lemon juice and the spinach. Stir well and cook, covered, over very low heat for about 18 minutes or until the rice is tender.

Serve hot or cold.

NOTE Frozen leaf spinach, defrosted and coarsely chopped, may be used.

1 LARGE ONION, CHOPPED

*100ML/ 3¹/₂ FL OZ/ ¹/₂ CUP
SUNFLOWER OIL*

4 TBSP PINE NUTS

*250G/ 9 OZ/ 1¹/₄ CUPS AMERICAN
LONG-GRAIN RICE*

SALT

¹/₂ TSP CINNAMON

¹/₄ TSP ALLSPICE

¹/₄ TSP GROUND CARDAMOM

*450ML/ 15 FL OZ/ 2 CUPS
VEGETABLE STOCK OR WATER*

2–3 TBSP CURRANTS OR RAISINS

VARIATION

Mix in at the end a small
tin of chick peas, drained,
boiled in water and then
drained again.

RICE PILAF WITH
RAISINS AND PINE NUTS

**This is the standard pilaf found in
Middle Eastern restaurants and cafeterias. It
makes a good side dish for many of the
vegetable dishes and can also be served cold.**

SERVES 4

Fry the onion in about half the oil over medium heat
until soft. Add the pine nuts and stir to brown them
lightly all over.

Add the rice and stir to coat the grains with oil.
Add salt, cinnamon, allspice and cardamom.

Cover with boiling stock or water, stir in the
currants or raisins and mix well. Cook, covered, for
18–20 minutes, until the rice is tender.

Stir in the remaining oil and serve hot or cold.

1 LARGE ONION, CHOPPED

50G/2 OZ/4 TBSP BUTTER

1 TBSP VEGETABLE OIL

300G/11 OZ/1½ CUPS RISOTTO RICE

500ML/18 FL OZ/2¼ CUPS DRY WHITE WINE

SALT AND PEPPER

500ML/18 FL OZ/2¼ CUPS VEGETABLE STOCK MADE WITH 1 STOCK (BOUILLON) CUBE

250G/9 OZ/2 CUPS PODDED BABY PEAS

250G/9 OZ ASPARAGUS TIPS

150ML/5 FL OZ/⅔ CUP DOUBLE (HEAVY) CREAM (OPTIONAL)

4 TBSP GRATED PARMESAN CHEESE (OPTIONAL)

VARIATION

Other vegetables could be added, such as sliced fennel or celery, sliced courgettes (zucchini) and broad (fava) beans.

RISOTTO WITH PEAS AND ASPARAGUS

This Italian springtime risotto is light and fresh. I prefer it without the cream and cheese but some of my family prefer the richer version. Serve it as a first course or as a main dish.

SERVES 4–6

In a large frying pan or sauté pan, fry the onion in half the amount of butter and all of the oil, over very low heat, until soft, stirring occasionally.

Add the rice, and stir until all the grains are coated with fat and become translucent. Pour in the white wine, season with salt and pepper and simmer gently until the wine is absorbed.

Gradually stir in the stock, a little at a time, adding more as it becomes absorbed, and water if necessary, until the rice is creamy but still *al dente*.

Meanwhile, cook the peas and asparagus in boiling salted water until they are just tender.

Stir the remaining butter, and the cream and cheese, if using, into the rice, and serve at once, topped with the drained vegetables.

COUSCOUS

Couscous is the indigenous Berber food of North Africa. The word refers to the hard semolina grain on which it is based as well as to the stew or soup and the side dishes that go with it. In North Africa, it is served at the end of a festive meal, before the sweet, or as a one-dish family meal. Stews and soups are nearly always based on meat or chicken, and sometimes fish (see Fish Couscous with Quince on page 167).
A stew with vegetables only is considered a dish *de regime* for people on a diet. But with a good assortment of vegetables, it can be a truly glorious affair – a joy to look at and a pleasure to eat. The combination of many different herbs and 'sweet' spices is part of the appeal.

BASIC METHOD FOR MAKING COUSCOUS

The couscous we get in Britain is a processed (pre-cooked) product. All you do is add salted water and oil and heat it through. When I visited a couscous factory in Sfax, Tunisia, the owner explained that their couscous could be heated in a saucepan, in the oven or the microwave.

I shamelessly make it the easiest way, as prescribed in the packet instructions, with very good results. It is so easy you can make it for very large parties. Simply measure the volume of the grain and add the same

LEFT *Vegetable Couscous (page 96)*

volume of warm water – even a little less, as you can add more later if necessary.

For 6 to 8 people put 500g/1lb/2½ cups medium-ground couscous in a bowl. Add 600ml/20fl oz/2½ cups warm water with ½–1 tsp salt, stirring slowly so that the water is absorbed evenly.

After about 10–15 minutes, when the couscous has become a little plump and tender, add 3–4 tbsp groundnut (peanut) or light vegetable oil and rub the grain between your hands to air it and break up any lumps. Heat it through by steaming in the top part of a couscoussier (it is ready as soon as the steam passes through the grain) or, more simply, in the oven, covered with foil, at 200°C/400°F/Gas 6 for about 20 minutes.

When I make couscous for a large number of people, I put it straight into the huge clay dish I plan to serve it in, which goes into the oven. There is nothing easier.

A small quantity for 2 or 3 people can be heated in a saucepan, stirring to prevent it from burning. Before serving, break up any lumps very thoroughly.

1 RECIPE GRILLED (BROILED)
OR ROASTED VEGETABLES (SEE
PAGE 102)

FOR THE BED OF COUSCOUS

500G/ 1 LB/ 2½ CUPS COUSCOUS

900ML/ 1½ PINTS/ 3¾ CUPS
WATER

1½ VEGETABLE STOCK (BOUILLON)
CUBES

A LITTLE SALT

1–2 GARLIC CLOVES, CRUSHED

½–1 TSP CINNAMON

¼ TSP ALLSPICE

¼ TSP POWDERED GINGER

¼ TSP SAFFRON (OPTIONAL)

A GOOD PINCH OF CHILLI POWDER

4 TBSP CHOPPED CORIANDER
(CILANTRO)

2 TBSP CHOPPED FLAT-LEAFED
PARSLEY

4 TBSP SUNFLOWER OR
VEGETABLE OIL

2 TBSP RAISINS, SOAKED IN WATER
FOR 10 MINUTES.

COUSCOUS WITH ROASTED VEGETABLES

This is not a traditional North African dish but it is most appealing.

SERVES 6

Pre-heat the oven to 200°C/400°F/Gas 6.

Prepare the vegetables – roast or grill (broil) them (see page 102). Re-heat them when you are about to serve.

Put the couscous in a large ovenproof serving dish.

Bring the water to the boil in a large pan. Add the stock cubes, salt (take into consideration the saltiness of the stock cubes), garlic, cinnamon, allspice, ginger, saffron and chilli powder. Simmer for 8 minutes until the garlic is soft. Remove from the heat and add the chopped coriander (cilantro) and parsley.

Pour 600ml/1 pint/2½ cups of this hot 'soup' over the couscous (keep the rest to moisten the grain when you are serving) and stir well so that it is absorbed evenly. Leave for 15 minutes or until the grain is tender. Stir in the oil and rub the grain between your palms to fluff it up and separate and break up any lumps, then drain the raisins and add them to the couscous.

About 20 minutes before serving, heat the grain through, covered with foil, in the oven.

Reheat the soup and the vegetables. Break up any lumps in the couscous and serve, with the remaining soup poured over and the hot vegetables on top.

FOR THE GARNISH

250G/ 9 OZ/ 1 1/4 CUPS CHICK PEAS,
SOAKED FOR AT LEAST 1 HOUR

SALT

150G/ 5 OZ/ 1 CUP RAISINS

FOR THE GRAIN

1 KG/ 2 LB/ 5 CUPS COUSCOUS

1.25 LITRES/ 2 PINTS/ 5 CUPS
WATER

1–2 TSP SALT

6 TBSP GROUNDNUT (PEANUT)
OR VEGETABLE OIL

AROMATICS

SALT AND PEPPER

2 TSP CINNAMON

1/2 TSP ALLSPICE

3/4 TSP GROUND GINGER

1/2 TSP SAFFRON POWDER

1/4 TSP CHILLI

A LARGE BUNCH (3/4 CUP) FLAT-
LEAFED PARSLEY, CHOPPED

A LARGE BUNCH (3/4 CUP)
CORIANDER (CILANTRO), CHOPPED

A BUNCH (1/2 CUP) ROCKET
(ARUGULA), COARSELY CHOPPED

A BUNCH (1/2 CUP) CRESS,
COARSELY CHOPPED

FOR THE PEPPERY SAUCE

2 TSP HARISSA (SEE PAGE 219)
OR MORE, TO TASTE, OR 2 TSP
PAPRIKA AND 1/4 –1/2 TSP OR MORE
CHILLI POWDER

VEGETABLE COUSCOUS

**The following recipe is for 10 or more
because it is as easy to make for many as it is for
a few and it is a good party dish. It can also be
made in advance. It might seem daunting because
of the number of ingredients but it is simply
a matter of throwing vegetables into a pot.
I give a long list of vegetables to choose from.
Seven is a usual number, but you can have as many
as you like and you can vary the quantities.**

SERVES 10–12

Pre-heat the oven to 200°C/400°F/Gas 6.

To make the garnish, boil the chick peas (garbanzo beans) in water for an hour or until tender, adding salt when they begin to soften. Boil the raisins separately for 15 minutes in enough water to cover.

Prepare the couscous grain as described on pages 93–4 in an ovenproof serving dish. About 20–30 minutes before serving, cover with foil and heat through in the oven (it will steam).

To prepare the stew or soup, put 2.5l/4½ pt/11½ cups water with 7 (or more) vegetables of your choice in a large saucepan. Bring to the boil and remove any scum. Add salt and pepper and the spices (but not the herbs) and simmer for 30 minutes or until all the vegetables are tender. Add the herbs and cook 5 more minutes.

To make the peppery sauce, put 2 ladlesful of liquid from the soup in a small bowl and stir in the Harissa or paprika and chilli powder.

VEGETABLES TO CHOOSE FROM FOR THE STEW OR SOUP

2 LARGE ONIONS, SLICED

500G/ 1 LB (ABOUT 4 LARGE) TURNIPS, CUT IN HALF OR LEFT WHOLE IF BABY ONES

500G/ 1 LB (ABOUT 4 LARGE) CARROTS, PEELED AND CUT IN HALF LENGTHWAYS

500G/ 1 LB (4 MEDIUM) POTATOES, PEELED AND QUARTERED

1 SMALL WHITE CABBAGE, CUT INTO 8 PIECES THROUGH THE HEART

3 RED (BELL) PEPPERS, CUT INTO RIBBONS

5 ARTICHOKE HEARTS, CUT IN HALF (YOU MAY USE FROZEN ONES)

3 SMALL FENNEL BULBS, QUARTERED

500G/ 1 LB BROAD (FAVA) BEANS OR PETITS POIS (YOU MAY USE FROZEN ONES)

4 MEDIUM TOMATOES, PEELED AND QUARTERED

500G/ 1 LB PIECE OF ORANGE PUMPKIN, CUT INTO 5CM/ 2 IN PIECES

500G/ 1 LB (ABOUT 3–4) COURGETTES (ZUCCHINI), CUT INTO 5 CM/ 2 IN SLICES OR IN HALF LENGTHWAYS

Before serving, break up any lumps in the couscous very thoroughly, stir in a little of the broth, and shape the grain into a little mountain. Serve the vegetables in a separate bowl or arrange them on top of the couscous. Reheat the chick peas and raisins, and put them into separate bowls. Put them on the table along with the peppery sauce, and let people help themselves.

MIXED VEGETABLE DISHES

The wide range of Mediterranean vegetables and the magnificent flavour they acquire under the warm sun are legendary. The art of cooking them the Mediterranean way – a rich amalgam of food traditions inherited from the ancient world, from the Byzantine and Ottoman Empires, the Arabs, France, Italy and Spain – has been carried to all the corners of the world. Many of the dishes in this section are ideal party food. They can be served as side dishes and they also make spectacular main dishes, served simply with bread and cheese.

FOR THE COOKING LIQUOR

1 BOTTLE (750ML/1¼ PINTS/ 3¼ CUPS) DRY WHITE WINE

175ML/6 FL OZ/¾ CUP VERY LIGHT, MILD-TASTING OR BLAND EXTRA VIRGIN OLIVE OIL

SALT TO TASTE

2 SPRIGS OF THYME

4 BAY LEAVES

SUGGESTIONS

You can use asparagus, spring onions (scallions), shiitake mushrooms, green beans, mange-tout (snow peas), tiny onions, carrots, potatoes, parsnips and turnips. To my surprise, my favourites for this treatment were carrots, potatoes and parsnips. Most vegetables are best left whole. Large carrots can be cut into thick slices or in half lengthwise, and turnips, parsnips and potatoes cut into slices or cubed.

VEGETABLES COOKED IN WHITE WINE AND OLIVE OIL

This Provençal method of cooking vegetables, in a mixture of white wine (I use a fruity dry Riesling) and olive oil, gives them a splendid flavour, and to some, a soft muted gold colour. They retain a certain firmness of texture even when they are long-cooked. A beautiful assortment makes a grand party dish to serve hot or cold. You must cook the vegetables in batches, giving each the time they require, which is longer than is needed in boiling water. Asparagus and spring onions (scallions), for instance, take about 10 minutes; carrots and potatoes 45–60 minutes. Let them bubble gently over low heat with the lid on.

Put the wine and oil in a large pan with some salt, thyme and bay leaves. Bring to the boil (oil will combine with the wine as the mixture bubbles) then simmer over low heat. Cook the vegetables in batches, lifting them out and arranging them on a serving platter as they become tender. If you want to serve them hot, heat through in the oven, covered with foil. I particularly like them cold.

2KG/4LB BABY VEGETABLES OR NEW SPRING VEGETABLES SUCH AS TINY NEW POTATOES, SPRING ONIONS (SCALLIONS), ASPARAGUS SPEARS, BABY COURGETTES (ZUCCHINI), TINY LEEKS, SMALL FENNEL BULBS AND CELERY HEARTS, PICKLING (PEARL) ONIONS, GREEN BEANS, MANGE-TOUT (SNOW PEAS), BABY LETTUCES AND SWEETCORN

ABOUT 2 LITRES/3¹/₂ PINTS/9 CUPS VEGETABLE STOCK — YOU MAY USE STOCK (BOUILLON) CUBES

SALT

2–3 GARLIC CLOVES, CHOPPED

4 BAY LEAVES

2 SPRIGS OF THYME

FOR THE DRESSING

100ML/3¹/₂ FL OZ/¹/₂ CUP VERY LIGHT MILD-TASTING OR BLAND EXTRA VIRGIN OLIVE OIL OR A MIXTURE OF OLIVE AND SUNFLOWER OIL

¹/₂ CUP MIXED CHOPPED HERBS, SUCH AS CHERVIL, CHIVES AND PARSLEY

VARIATION

To intensify the flavour you might like to add the juice of ¹/₂ lemon and 1 tbsp granulated sugar to the stock.

BABY VEGETABLES COOKED IN STOCK

About 10 years ago the chefs of Provence brought into fashion tiny baby vegetables and have since refined their ways of cooking them. If the variety of vegetables is large enough, you can serve the dish as the main part of a meal for four, or pile them onto a platter as the centrepiece for a dinner party. Perfectionists boil the vegetables separately as they cook at slightly different rates, even though they are all tiny.

SERVES 4

Leave the vegetables whole. Wash them, peel them (or not, as desired), but leave the little stalks and leaves if they have them. Trim the roots and dark green ends of leeks and spring onions (scallions). Boil the vegetables in enough stock to cover, with salt if necessary, the garlic cloves, bay leaves and thyme, until *al dente*. Drain.

Make a dressing by mixing together the oil and herbs and pour over the vegetables.

1 LARGE AUBERGINE (EGGPLANT), CUT INTO 1–1.25 CM/ $^{1}/_{3}$ –$^{1}/_{2}$ IN SLICES LENGTHWAYS

SALT

4 MEDIUM COURGETTES (ZUCCHINI), CUT INTO 1–1.25 CM/ $^{1}/_{3}$ –$^{1}/_{2}$ IN SLICES LENGTHWAYS

2 MEDIUM MILD ONIONS, CUT INTO THICK SLICES

2–4 PLUM TOMATOES, CUT IN HALF

2 RED OR YELLOW (BELL) PEPPERS, CUT IN HALF

EXTRA VIRGIN OLIVE OIL

4–8 FAT GARLIC CLOVES IN THEIR SKINS

PEPPER

4 TBSP CHOPPED HERBS SUCH AS PARSLEY, BASIL, CHERVIL OR MARJORAM (OPTIONAL)

VARIATIONS

If you serve the vegetables cold, you may like to squeeze a little lemon juice over them or sprinkle with a little sherry or balsamic vinegar.

For pasta with grilled (broiled) or roasted vegetables, boil 400g/14oz pasta in salted water until al dente, then drain. Dress with 6 tbsp or more extra virgin olive oil mixed with 6 tbsp chopped flat-leafed parsley and serve topped with the roasted vegetables.

GRILLED (BROILED) OR ROASTED VEGETABLES

Vegetables cooked on a barbecue or under the grill (broiler), or roasted at high heat in the oven, develop a rich intense flavour. All kinds of vegetables may be grilled (broiled), but those listed (left) are a typical Mediterranean combination.
This recipe makes a wonderful meal in itself.
The same roasted vegetables can be served over a couscous base (see page 96) or with pasta.

SERVES 4

Sprinkle the aubergine (eggplant) slices with salt and leave them to degorge their bitter juices for 30 minutes, then rinse and dry them.

Brush the aubergine (eggplant), onions, courgettes (zucchini), tomatoes and peppers with oil.

Cook the aubergine (eggplant), onions and courgettes (zucchini) on the barbecue or under the grill (broiler) until tender and browned, turning them over once. Do the peppers with the skin side only towards the fire. Be sure the aubergines (eggplants) are properly cooked – when underdone they are unpleasant (they are ready when they feel very soft when you prick them with a fork). Cook the tomatoes and garlic cloves until softened.

Alternatively, roast the sliced vegetables on trays lined with foil in a very hot (250°C/480°F/Gas 10) oven, being careful that they do not overcook.

Arrange all the vegetables on a serving plate. The garlic cloves can be peeled or left in their skins.

Serve hot or cold, sprinkled with salt and pepper, a drizzle of olive oil and, if you like, chopped parsley or other fresh herbs such as basil, chervil or marjoram.

2 MEDIUM AUBERGINES
(EGGPLANTS)

2 MEDIUM ONIONS

2 RED (BELL) PEPPERS

2 PLUM TOMATOES

1 WHOLE HEAD OF GARLIC WITH
FAT CLOVES

4–5 TBSP OLIVE OIL

SALT AND PEPPER

WHOLE ROASTED VEGETABLES

**This is another popular way of cooking vegetables
in the Mediterranean – a plateful served with
an assortment of good cheeses makes a perfect meal.**

SERVES 4

Pre-heat the oven to 180°C/350°F/Gas 4.

Prick the aubergines (eggplants) with a sharp knife to prevent them bursting. Put all the vegetables whole, as they are, on baking trays lined with foil. Roast them in the oven until soft. Take the tomatoes and garlic out after 20 minutes, when they soften. Leave the onions, peppers and aubergines (eggplants) in for about 1 hour until the skins are brown, turning them once.

Drop the peppers into a thick polythene bag and twist to seal it (this loosens the skin). When they are cool enough to handle, peel the vegetables and deseed the peppers. Cut the tomatoes in half, the onions in quarters, the (bell) peppers and aubergines (eggplants) into strips. Peel the garlic cloves and leave them whole.

Dress with the olive oil, salt and pepper and mix together. Serve cold.

4 SMALL TURNIPS

1 LARGE PARSNIP

1 LARGE CARROT

1 SWEET POTATO (ABOUT 250G/ 9 OZ)

2 TBSP SUNFLOWER OR VEGETABLE OIL

STOCK MADE WITH 500ML/ 18 FL OZ/ 2¼ CUPS WATER MIXED WITH 1 VEGETABLE STOCK (BOUILLON) CUBE

100 ML/ 3½ FL OZ/ 1½ CUP DRY WHITE WINE (OPTIONAL)

SALT AND PEPPER

1 TBSP LEMON JUICE

16 CHESTNUTS

ROOT VEGETABLES WITH CHESTNUTS

It is worth making use of chestnuts in this engaging French way. You may use either frozen or vacuum-packed ones.

SERVES 4

Peel the vegetables and cut them into 2.5cm/1in cubes and put them in a pan.

Pour in the oil, stock and wine to cover. Season with salt and plenty of pepper, taking into consideration the saltiness of the stock, and add the lemon juice.

Simmer, uncovered, for about 25 minutes, or until the vegetables are just tender and the liquid is reduced to a sauce.

Meanwhile, prepare the chestnuts. To peel them, make a slit in their flat side with a pointed knife and roast them under the grill (broiler) for 2 minutes, turning them over once, until they blacken slightly. Peel them as soon as they are cool enough to handle. Drop them into the pan with the vegetables and cook in the sauce for 5 minutes or longer. Raise the heat to high, if necessary, to reduce the sauce.

Serve hot.

FOR THE BATTER

150G/ 5 OZ/ 1 CUP PLAIN (ALL-
PURPOSE) FLOUR

1/2 TSP SALT

1 TSP BAKING POWDER

1 TBSP EXTRA VIRGIN OLIVE OIL

1 EGG YOLK, SIZE 1 (U.S. LARGE)

ABOUT 200ML/ 7 FL OZ/ 3/4 CUP
WATER OR SODA WATER

FOR THE VEGETABLES

CHOOSE A VARIETY FROM THE
FOLLOWING: FAT SPRING ONIONS
(SCALLIONS), TRIMMED OF THEIR
ROOTS AND DARK GREEN ENDS;
ASPARAGUS (TRIMMED OF THEIR
TOUGH ENDS); BUTTON
MUSHROOMS; COURGETTES
(ZUCCHINI), SLICED LENGTHWAYS;
AUBERGINES (EGGPLANTS), SLICED
INTO ROUNDS 1 CM/ 1/2 IN THICK;
CAULIFLOWER, BOILED FIRST THEN
CUT INTO FLORETS; ARTICHOKE
BOTTOMS, CUT INTO SLICES

SUNFLOWER OR VEGETABLE OIL
FOR DEEP FRYING

SALT AND PEPPER

1 LEMON, CUT INTO WEDGES

MIXED VEGETABLE FRITTERS

**Italians are famous for their deep-fried
vegetables in batter – *fritti misti di verdura* – which
vary in content from one region to another and
to which, in the south, they sometimes add egg-and-
breadcrumbed pieces of mozzarella, and in the
north, lumps of fried, slightly sweet, thick 'cream'
(actually milk cooked with ground rice) and
pieces of fruit such as sliced apple. But every other
country in the Mediterranean has some version
of vegetable fritters too. Turks specialize in fried
aubergine (eggplant) and courgette (zucchini)
slices, which they serve with yoghurt or with a fresh
Tomato Sauce (see page 218).**

To make the batter, mix the flour, salt and baking
powder in a large bowl, and add the oil and egg yolk.
Vigorously beat in enough water to make a light creamy
batter. Leave to rest for 30 minutes and beat again
before using.

To make the fritters, cut the vegetables into slices,
dip them in the batter and deep-fry in sizzling, medium-
hot sunflower oil until crisp and lightly browned and
tender inside. Drain on paper towels.

Serve at once, sprinkled with salt and pepper, and
accompanied with lemon wedges. Re-heat, if necessary,
in the oven.

OVERLEAF *From left to right:*
*Mixed Vegetable Fritters; Spaghetti with (Bell) Peppers
and Aubergines (Eggplants) (page 75)*

500G/ 1 LB (ABOUT 5) SMALL
TURNIPS, PEELED

200G/ 7 OZ/ 1 ¾ CUPS SHELLED
BROAD (FAVA) BEANS

1 GARLIC CLOVE, FINELY CHOPPED

3 TBSP SUNFLOWER OR
VEGETABLE OIL

JUICE OF ½ LEMON

1–2 TSP GRANULATED SUGAR

1 TSP DRIED MINT

ABOUT 4 TBSP WATER

250G/ 9 OZ SPINACH

BROAD (FAVA) BEANS, TURNIPS AND SPINACH

It is best to use fresh vegetables but frozen broad (fava) beans and frozen whole leaf spinach will do very well.

SERVES 4–6

Cut the turnips in half then into 1cm/⅓in thick slices. Put them in a large pan with the beans, garlic and oil, and sauté over very low heat for 5–10 minutes until lightly coloured.

Add the lemon juice, sugar, mint and water and cook for about 10–20 minutes, until the vegetables are tender.

Meanwhile, wash and drain the spinach (remove the stems only if they are tough), and press out the excess water. When the beans and turnips have almost finished cooking, add the spinach to the pan. Put the lid on so that the leaves cook in the steam for a minute or two, until they crumple. Stir well and adjust the seasoning.

Serve hot or cold.

NOTE If using frozen beans and spinach, simply defrost and add to the pan when the turnips are tender, then cook for a few more minutes.

OMELETTES AND EGG DISHES

The Mediterranean is famous for its egg dishes and omelettes. The latter are usually like thick cakes, filled with vegetables, and can be eaten hot or cold. Accompanied with salad they make a good family meal, and because they can be made in advance, they are an easy option for entertaining and buffet meals. They are colourful and can look quite elegant, cut into wedges or little squares and garnished with cress. They are also traditional picnic foods.

250G/ 9 OZ SPINACH (YOU MAY USE FROZEN LEAF SPINACH)

1 LARGE ONION, CHOPPED

4 TBSP SUNFLOWER OR LIGHT VEGETABLE OIL

1 LARGE TOMATO, PEELED AND CHOPPED

SALT AND PEPPER

4 EGGS, SIZE 1 (U.S. LARGE)

1/4 TSP NUTMEG

VARIATIONS

A handful of cooked chick peas (garbanzo beans) or white haricot (navy) beans may be added to the omelette mixture.

For a Provençal omelette, cook 400g/14oz spinach and mix with 4 large eggs, a pinch of nutmeg, 1 crushed garlic clove and 4 tbsp grated Parmesan or Gruyère cheese.

Another French version adds a handful of cooked green peas and 2 artichoke hearts cut into slices.

SPINACH OMELETTE

Every Arab country has a version of spinach omelette. This one is Egyptian.

SERVES 4

Wash and drain the fresh spinach and squeeze the water out between your hands. Remove the stems only if they are tough. Put it in a saucepan over a low heat and cover with the lid. The spinach will cook in the steam of the water that clings to it and crumple very quickly to a soft mass. Drain in a colander and press all the water out.

If using frozen spinach, thaw thoroughly and press all the water out.

Fry the onion in 2 tbsp of the oil until golden. Add the tomato, salt and pepper and cook for 15 minutes or until the sauce is reduced.

Beat the eggs lightly in a bowl with salt, pepper and nutmeg. Add the tomato sauce and the spinach, and mix well.

Heat the rest of the oil in a frying pan (preferably a non-stick pan). Pour in the spinach and egg mixture and cook over a low heat for about 10 minutes until the bottom of the omelette sets firm. Put the pan under the grill (broiler) and cook until the top of the omelette is firm and lightly browned.

Serve hot or cold, cut into wedges.

750G/ 1 ½ LB (ABOUT 2 MEDIUM)
AUBERGINES (EGGPLANTS)

1 LARGE ONION, CHOPPED

4 TBSP OLIVE OIL

3 GARLIC CLOVES, CRUSHED

4 EGGS, SIZE 1 (U.S. LARGE)

½ CUP COARSELY CHOPPED FLAT-
LEAFED PARSLEY

½–1 TSP GROUND CARAWAY SEEDS

½ TSP GROUND CORIANDER

SALT AND PEPPER

1 LEMON, CUT INTO WEDGES

AUBERGINE (EGGPLANT) OMELETTE

Maacoudes – omelettes that combine all kinds of ingredients – are among the most popular hors-d'oeuvres in Tunisia. They are served hot or cold. This one has a lovely, subtle texture and flavour.

SERVES 4

Prick the aubergines (eggplants) in a few places with a pointed knife to prevent them from bursting. Put them on a baking tray under the grill (broiler) for about 20 minutes, turning them until their skin is black and the flesh feels soft when you press them.

Fry the onion in 2 tbsp of the oil over a very low heat until golden, stirring occasionally. Add the garlic and stir until lightly coloured.

Put the aubergines (eggplants) in a colander and peel them. Chop the flesh with two knives in the colander, then mash it with a fork, allowing the juices to run out.

In a bowl, beat the eggs lightly. Add the mashed aubergine (eggplant), the onion, garlic, parsley, caraway, coriander, salt and pepper. Mix well.

Heat the remaining oil in a large, preferably non-stick, frying pan. Pour in the mixture and cook, covered, over a very low heat for about 10 minutes until the bottom has set. Put the frying pan under the grill (broiler) and cook until the top is firm and lightly browned.

Serve hot or cold accompanied with lemon wedges.

1 ONION, COARSELY CHOPPED

6 TBSP EXTRA VIRGIN OLIVE OIL, OR
AS REQUIRED

2 GARLIC CLOVES, CHOPPED

1 MEDIUM AUBERGINE (EGGPLANT),
CUT INTO 1.5 CM/ 2/3 IN CUBES

2 MEDIUM COURGETTES
(ZUCCHINI), CUT INTO 1.25 CM/
1/2 IN SLICES

1 RED (BELL) PEPPER, CUT INTO
1.5 CM/ 2/3 IN STRIPS

4 MEDIUM TOMATOES, PEELED
AND CHOPPED

SALT AND PEPPER

1 TSP GRANULATED SUGAR

1 SPRIG OF THYME, CRUMBLED

4 TBSP CHOPPED PARSLEY

4 EGGS, SIZE 1 (U.S. LARGE),
LIGHTLY BEATEN

VARIATION

Break the eggs over the
vegetables and cook them
whole.

FIVE VEGETABLE OMELETTE

In the south of France this dish is called a
tian de bohemienne. In North Africa a mixture of
fried vegetables with eggs in a frying pan
is a *shakshouka*. All kinds of vegetables can go into
a *shakshouka*, including peas, broad (fava) beans
and pumpkin, but the most popular combination is
that usually found in ratatouille. The French
deep-fry the vegetables separately then drain them,
mix them with the rest of the ingredients and
bake them, but sautéing them all in the frying pan
is quicker and equally good.

SERVES 4

In a large frying pan, fry the onion in 2 tbsp of the oil until soft.

Add the garlic, aubergine (eggplant), courgettes (zucchini), (bell) pepper and the rest of the oil and sauté, over high then medium heat, turning the vegetables over frequently, until lightly coloured.

Add the tomatoes, salt, pepper, sugar and thyme, and cook until the vegetables are tender.

Add the parsley and eggs, a little more salt and pepper, stir very gently, and cook until the eggs have set.

Serve hot with bread.

2 LARGE POTATOES, PEELED AND CUT INTO 0.5 CM/ ¼ IN SLICES

1 LARGE SPANISH ONION, THINLY SLICED

SALT

125 ML/ 4 FL OZ/ ½ CUP OIL – A MIXTURE OF OLIVE OIL AND LIGHT VEGETABLE OIL

3 EGGS, SIZE 1 (U.S. LARGE), LIGHTLY BEATEN

SPANISH POTATO TORTILLA

The tortilla is the most popular appetizer served in Spanish bars, but it can also be the centre of a family meal. It can be made in advance and re-heated or eaten cold.

SERVES 4–5

Sprinkle the potatoes and onion lightly with salt.

Heat the oil in a non-stick frying pan and add the potatoes and onions at the same time. Cook slowly over a medium heat (it is really stewing rather than frying), for about 15 minutes, stirring occasionally, until the vegetables are tender but not brown.

Drain the vegetables in a colander, reserving the oil.

In a bowl, mix the potatoes and onion with the eggs and leave to soak for about 15 minutes.

Wipe the frying pan clean and heat 2 tbsp of the reserved oil to sizzling hot. Pour in the potato and egg mixture and lower the heat to medium-low. Shake the pan occasionally to prevent the tortilla from sticking. When it starts to come away from the sides of the pan and the bottom has browned a little, turn over the tortilla by placing a large plate over the frying pan and quickly turning the tortilla upside-down onto it. Add another tablespoon of oil to the frying pan and quickly slide the tortilla back in. Cook the other side for a minute. Alternatively, brown under the grill (broiler).

Serve hot or cold, cut into wedges.

3 GARLIC CLOVES, OR TO TASTE, CHOPPED

3 TBSP SUNFLOWER OR EXTRA VIRGIN OLIVE OIL

4 PLUM TOMATOES, CUT INTO 1 CM/ $^1/_3$ IN SLICES

SALT AND PEPPER

$^2/_3$ TSP GRANULATED SUGAR

4 EGGS, SIZE 1 (U.S. LARGE)

3 TBSP CHOPPED BASIL, CORIANDER (CILANTRO) OR PARSLEY

VARIATIONS

Peel and chop the tomatoes. Cook as described (right) and when they have softened, add the eggs and scramble them gently. Serve them soft and creamy.

Add a few pitted black olives, cut into pieces.

EGG AND TOMATO

When one of my children arrives unexpectedly at meal time, Egg and Tomato is one of the things I rustle up. It is a common standby in Egypt. Often, I do not bother to peel the tomatoes, and it makes no difference to the end result.

SERVES 2

In a large frying pan, fry the garlic in the oil until it begins to colour.

Add the tomatoes, preferably in one layer, and season lightly with salt, pepper and sugar. Cook for 2–3 minutes then turn over the tomato slices.

Break open the eggs on top of the tomatoes and sprinkle with salt and pepper. Cook over gentle heat until the eggs have set.

Serve hot, sprinkled with the chopped herbs. Accompany with bread.

2 RED (BELL) PEPPERS

1 MEDIUM ONION, CHOPPED

2 TBSP OLIVE OR SUNFLOWER OIL

500G/1 LB (ABOUT 6 MEDIUM)
TOMATOES, PEELED AND DICED

SALT AND PEPPER

1–2 TSP GRANULATED SUGAR

2 TBSP CAPERS (OPTIONAL)

1/2–1 TSP HARISSA (SEE PAGE 219)
OR 1 TSP PAPRIKA AND A GOOD
PINCH OF CAYENNE OR RED CHILLI
POWDER (OPTIONAL)

4 EGGS, SIZE 1 (U.S. LARGE),
LIGHTLY BEATEN

VARIATIONS

To make it a substantial
dish, add 2 boiled, peeled
and diced potatoes or a
drained 400g/14oz tin of
white haricot (navy) beans.

You may also add a handful
of grated Gruyère or
crumbled feta.

EGGS BAKED WITH (BELL) PEPPERS AND TOMATOES

This delectable Tunisian dish is called a *tagine* after the shallow clay dish in which it is cooked.

SERVES 4

Pre-heat the oven to 180°C/350°F/Gas 4.

Grill (broil) the (bell) peppers (for directions see page 216), peel and cut the flesh into ribbons.

Fry the onion in the oil until golden. Add the tomatoes, salt, pepper and sugar and simmer for about 20 minutes until the sauce is reduced.

Remove from the heat and add the capers, the Harissa, diluted in a tablespoon of water, or the paprika and cayenne.

Let the mixture cool a little, then beat in the eggs.

Put the peppers in an oiled baking dish (about 23cm/9in diameter) and pour the egg mixture on top. Bake for 50 minutes or until set. Serve hot.

FLANS, GRATINS AND CHEESE BAKES

These baked vegetable dishes with eggs and cheese make ideal vegetarian meals because they contain all the necessary proteins, carbohydrates, fibre and nutrients. They are also extremely satisfying and have an added advantage in that they can be made in advance and reheated before serving. French *tians* and Italian *pasticcios* are creamy, with a béchamel base, while the Arab equivalents are often made with eggs. Serve them as main dishes, accompanied with salad. They are delicious both hot and cold and are perfect for buffet meals.

1 LARGE ONION, CHOPPED

1 1/2 TBSP OLIVE OIL

4 EGGS, SIZE 1 (U.S. LARGE)

125ML/4 FL OZ/ 1/2 CUP MILK

SALT AND WHITE PEPPER

A PINCH OF NUTMEG

500G/1 LB (ABOUT 4 LARGISH) COURGETTES (ZUCCHINI), VERY THINLY SLICED

FOR THE SAUCE

1–2 GARLIC CLOVES, FINELY CHOPPED

1 TBSP OLIVE OIL

500G/1 LB (ABOUT 6 MEDIUM) TOMATOES, PEELED AND CHOPPED

SALT AND PEPPER

1–2 TSP GRANULATED SUGAR

1–2 TBSP COARSELY CHOPPED BLACK OLIVES

1–2 TBSP CAPERS, SQUEEZED TO REMOVE EXCESS VINEGAR

COURGETTE (ZUCCHINI) CAKE WITH TOMATO SAUCE

The olives and capers in the sauce lift the delicate flavours of the courgettes (zucchini) and creamy custard of this Provençal flan.

SERVES 4

Pre-heat the oven to 180°C/350°F/Gas 4.

Fry the onion in the oil over medium heat until very soft and golden, stirring often. Set aside.

Beat the eggs lightly with a fork, then beat in the milk and add salt, pepper and nutmeg. Add the fried onions and the courgettes (zucchini) and mix well.

Pour into a 26cm/10in well-greased flan mould or baking dish. Bake for 1½ hours or until firm (cover with foil for the first hour so that the top does not over-brown).

Meanwhile, prepare the sauce. Fry the garlic in the oil over low heat, stirring, until slightly coloured. Add the tomatoes, salt, pepper and sugar and simmer for 20 minutes until reduced. Add the olives and capers and cook for a few more minutes.

Serve the courgette (zucchini) cake with the sauce poured over.

1 LARGE ONION, COARSELY
CHOPPED

2 TBSP SUNFLOWER OR VEGETABLE
OIL

750G / 1 1/2 LB COURGETTES
(ZUCCHINI), CUT INTO 1 CM / 1/3 IN
SLICES

SALT

3 EGGS, SIZE 1 (U.S. LARGE),
LIGHTLY BEATEN

200G / 7 OZ GRATED (MEDIUM)
CHEDDAR CHEESE

WHITE PEPPER

A FEW GRATINGS OF NUTMEG

COURGETTE (ZUCCHINI) GRATIN

This is a dish from the Arab Mediterranean where it is often served with yoghurt. I have substituted Cheddar for the usual feta cheese because it complements the courgettes (zucchini) particularly well.

SERVES 4

Pre-heat the oven to 180°C/350°F/Gas 4.

Fry the onion in the oil over medium heat until golden. Next, poach the courgettes (zucchini) in salted water for a few minutes only (they should be slightly underdone) and drain.

Mix the eggs with the fried onions and cheese, add pepper and nutmeg, and fold in the courgettes (zucchini).

Pour into a greased baking dish and bake for about 30 minutes or until set and lightly browned.

750G/ 1 1/2 LB AUBERGINES
(EGGPLANTS), CUT INTO 1 CM/
1/3 IN SLICES

SALT

1 LARGE ONION, CHOPPED

SUNFLOWER OIL FOR FRYING

750G/ 1 1/2 LB TOMATOES, PEELED
AND CHOPPED

2 TSP GRANULATED SUGAR

200G/ 7 OZ FONTINA CHEESE,
THINLY SLICED

500ML/ 18 FL OZ/ 2 1/4 CUPS MILK

4 EGGS, SIZE 1 (U.S. LARGE)

2 TBSP GRATED PARMESAN CHEESE

PEPPER

AUBERGINE (EGGPLANT), TOMATO AND FONTINA CHEESE FLAN

This *pasticcio di melanzane* hails from southern Italy.

SERVES 6

Soak the aubergines (eggplants) for 30 minutes in water with plenty of salt. Rinse, drain and dry them.

To make a tomato sauce, fry the onion in 2 tbsp of oil until golden. Add the tomatoes, salt, pepper and sugar and cook for 15–20 minutes.

Pre-heat the oven to 180°C/350°F/Gas 4.

Deep-fry the aubergine (eggplant) slices in hot oil very briefly, turning them over once, until slightly browned, then drain on paper towels. Alternatively, you can grill (broil) the slices – brush them generously with oil, arrange them on an oven tray and cook them under a hot grill (broiler), turning to brown them on both sides.

In a baking dish, put layers of aubergine (eggplant), Fontina cheese and tomato sauce.

Beat the milk with the eggs and Parmesan, add salt and pepper and pour over the dish.

Bake for 1 1/4 hours or until set. Serve hot.

1 RECIPE TOMATO SAUCE (SEE PAGE 218)

500G/1 LB (1 LARGE OR 2 MEDIUM) AUBERGINES (EGGPLANTS), CUT INTO ROUND 1 CM/1/3 IN SLICES

SALT

VEGETABLE OR SUNFLOWER OIL FOR FRYING

PEPPER

4 TBSP CHOPPED FLAT-LEAFED PARSLEY

100G/4 OZ FETA CHEESE, MASHED WITH A FORK

3 EGGS, SIZE 1 (U.S. LARGE)

VARIATIONS

For a *parmigiana di melanzane*, use a small bunch of torn basil leaves instead of the parsley. Instead of feta, top with 2 balls (250g/9oz) diced mozzarella cheese and 6 tbsp grated Parmesan (with no eggs).

A French version uses béchamel sauce mixed with grated Gruyère as the topping.

BAKED AUBERGINES (EGGPLANTS) WITH TOMATO SAUCE AND FETA CHEESE

This is the Arab equivalent of the famous Italian *parmigiana di melanzane*.

SERVES 4

Pre-heat the oven to 200°C/400°F/Gas 6.

Make the tomato sauce as directed on page 218.

Sprinkle the aubergine (eggplant) with salt and leave for 30 minutes until the juices are drawn out. Then rinse off the salt and dry with paper towels. Fry the slices very briefly in very hot oil (so that they absorb as little oil as possible), turning them over once, until browned. Drain on paper towels and arrange on the bottom of a 28cm/11in baking dish.

Sprinkle with pepper and parsley and spoon a layer of tomato sauce over them.

Beat the feta cheese with the eggs until well blended and spoon this mixture over the tomato sauce.

Bake for 20–30 minutes until set. Serve hot.

750G/ 1 1/2 LB ORANGE PUMPKIN, PEELED AND CUT INTO PIECES

SALT AND WHITE PEPPER

A PINCH OF NUTMEG

1 SMALL ONION, CHOPPED

1 TBSP BUTTER

1 TBSP VEGETABLE OIL

1 TBSP PLAIN (ALL-PURPOSE) FLOUR

250ML/ 8 FL OZ/ 1 CUP MILK

2 EGGS, SIZE 1 (U.S. LARGE), LIGHTLY BEATEN

2–3 TBSP GRATED GRUYÈRE CHEESE

BAKED PUMPKIN CREAM

**This creamy *tian de courge* of the Vaucluse
in the south of France has a sweet, delicate flavour
that everyone loves. It can be served as a first
course or as a main dish if accompanied by a fresh
Tomato Sauce (see page 218).
You need the orange-fleshed pumpkin that you
find in Indian, Greek and Middle Eastern
stores almost throughout the year. They are very
large and are sold by the slice with
seeds and fibres removed.**

SERVES 4

Pre-heat the oven to 200°C/400°F/Gas 6.

Put the pumpkin in a pan with about 4 tablespoons water. Put the lid on and steam for about 15 minutes until very soft. Mash with a potato masher or fork, and add salt, pepper and nutmeg. Cook, stirring, over medium heat for a few minutes, until most of the liquid has evaporated (pumpkin releases a lot of water).

Fry the onion in the butter and oil over medium heat until soft but not brown. Add the flour and cook, stirring, for a minute or so.

Gradually add the milk, a little at a time, stirring to prevent lumps from forming, and cook over low heat until the white sauce thickens.

Mix the sauce with the pumpkin and the eggs, and beat well. Pour into a well-buttered 23cm/9in baking dish. Sprinkle with grated Gruyère and bake for 40 minutes or until the top is slightly firm and golden.

750G/1 1/2 LB ORANGE PUMPKIN (WEIGHT WITH SKIN BUT WITHOUT SEEDS AND FIBRES)

ABOUT 5 TBSP WATER

2 EGGS, SIZE 1 (U.S. LARGE), LIGHTLY BEATEN

100G/4 OZ FETA CHEESE, MASHED

4 TBSP GRATED PARMESAN CHEESE

PUMPKIN GRATIN

This recipe is from the Eastern Mediterranean.

SERVES 4

Pre-heat the oven to 180°C/350°F/Gas 4.

Peel the pumpkin and cut it into pieces. Put the pieces in a pan with the water and steam, with the lid on, for 15 minutes or until very soft. (Pumpkin will release quite a lot of liquid.) Mash it with a fork and cook over medium heat, stirring, for a few minutes until most of the liquid has evaporated.

Beat the eggs with the feta and Parmesan, then mix with the pumpkin. The cheeses are salty and you should not need to add extra salt, but taste to find out.

Pour into a greased 20cm/8in baking dish and bake for about 25 minutes or until firm.

400G/14 OZ FRESH OR FROZEN
SPINACH

1/2 ONION, CHOPPED

25G/1 OZ/2 TBSP BUTTER

2 TBSP PLAIN (ALL-PURPOSE)
FLOUR

300ML/10 FL OZ/1 1/4 CUPS
BOILING MILK

SALT AND PEPPER

A PINCH OF NUTMEG

2 EGGS, SIZE 1 (U.S. LARGE),
LIGHTLY BEATEN

2 HARD-BOILED EGGS, SIZE 1 (U.S.
LARGE), CUT INTO PIECES

50G/2 OZ GRATED GRUYÈRE

VARIATION

Use a mixture of sorrel or
other green leaves such as
lettuce with the spinach,
and add a few pitted black
olives.

BAKED SPINACH WITH EGGS AND CHEESE

**This *tian d'epinards*, a speciality of the Vaucluse,
is a homely, satisfying dish.**

SERVES 4

Pre-heat the oven to 200°C/400°F/Gas 6.

If using fresh spinach, wash and drain it (remove
the stems only if they are hard). Cook the leaves in a
covered pan with no added water (they steam in the
water that clings to them) until they crumple. Drain in a
colander, reserving the juice. If using frozen whole leaf
spinach, defrost and press out the excess water.

In a pan, fry the onion in the butter over low
heat until soft. Add the flour and stir. Gradually stir
in the milk and the
spinach juice and cook
for 5 minutes, stirring
constantly to prevent
lumps from forming.

Add salt, pepper
and nutmeg, the lightly
beaten eggs and the
spinach, and beat well.

Fold in the hard-boiled eggs and the Gruyère and
pour into a greased 23 cm (9 in) baking dish. Bake for 40
minutes or until slightly firm and golden on top.

VEGETABLE SIDE DISHES

Anyone who has walked through a Mediterranean vegetable market knows how enthralling an experience it can be, with so much colourful fresh produce to choose from. Side dishes in Mediterranean countries are not the tasteless boiled or steamed vegetables we are used to here. They can be beguiling, yet simple at the same time. Serve them with egg dishes, flans and gratins, or with fish.

750G/ 1 1/2 LB BABY NEW POTATOES

2 WHOLE HEADS OF GARLIC, CUT IN HALF CROSSWISE

3 BAY LEAVES

3 SPRIGS OF THYME

1 FRESH CHILLI PEPPER

SALT AND PEPPER

EXTRA VIRGIN OLIVE OIL

HERBY NEW POTATOES

In this traditional Provençal method of cooking potatoes, they are boiled with garlic and herbs and absorb the flavours through their skins. I like to use the tiny new potatoes now available in our supermarkets. Bring them to the table with the halved garlic heads, which are good to eat, and the sprigs of herbs.

SERVES 4

Rinse and scrub the potatoes. Put them in a pan with enough water to cover and add the rest of the ingredients, except the pepper and the oil.

Simmer until the potatoes are tender. Leave them in the cooking water to absorb the flavours until you are ready to serve.

Drain and serve, hot or cold, with a drizzle of olive oil and a sprinkling of salt and pepper.

750G/ 1 1/2 LB (ABOUT 4 LARGE)
FLOURY POTATOES

SALT AND PEPPER

6 TBSP EXTRA VIRGIN OLIVE OIL

4 TBSP CHOPPED FLAT-LEAFED
PARSLEY

MASHED POTATOES WITH
OLIVE OIL AND PARSLEY

**This dish can be eaten hot
or cold and goes well with fish.**

SERVES 4

Peel the potatoes and boil them in salted water until soft. Drain, reserving about 100ml/3½fl oz/½ cup of the cooking water.

Mash the potatoes. Beat in the olive oil, add salt and pepper to taste and enough of the cooking water to achieve a soft, slightly moist texture. Stir in the parsley and serve hot.

VARIATION

Add 3 tbsp capers or chopped pitted black olives and fold them in.

1 ONION, CHOPPED

2 TBSP EXTRA VIRGIN OLIVE OIL

2 GARLIC CLOVES, CHOPPED

400G/ 14 OZ TOMATOES (ABOUT
5–6), PEELED AND CHOPPED

2 TSP GRANULATED SUGAR

SALT AND PEPPER

2 SPRIGS OF THYME, CHOPPED

750G/ 1 1/2 LB NEW POTATOES,
CUT INTO 2 CM/ 3/4 IN CUBES

ABOUT 200ML/ 7 FL OZ/ 3/4 CUP
VEGETABLE STOCK (YOU MAY USE
1/2 STOCK (BOUILLON) CUBE
DISSOLVED IN 3/4 CUP WATER)

2 TBSP CHOPPED FLAT-LEAFED
PARSLEY

POTATOES STEWED IN FRESH
TOMATO SAUCE

I discovered this potato dish in Provence.

SERVES 4

Fry the onion in the oil until golden. Add the garlic and cook, stirring, until the aroma rises.

Add the tomatoes, sugar, salt, pepper and thyme, and simmer for about 15 minutes. Put in the potatoes, cover with stock, and simmer gently until the potatoes are tender and the sauce has reduced. Stir in the parsley and serve.

375G/13 OZ FRESH SPINACH

150ML/5 FL OZ/²/₃ CUP DOUBLE
(HEAVY) CREAM

1 EGG, SIZE 1 (U.S. LARGE)

SALT AND PEPPER

SPINACH MOUSSE

**This wonderfully creamy French mousse can be served
with fish or as a first course with Fresh Tomato Sauce
(see page 218) and a sprinkling of Parmesan.
It is equally delicious served hot, with a hot sauce,
or cold with a cold sauce.**

SERVES 4

Pre-heat the oven to 180°C/350°F/Gas 4.

Wash the spinach and remove the stems only if they are tough. Drain and press out the excess water. Put the leaves in a pan and cook, covered, over low heat until they crumple into a soft mass. (They will steam in the water that clings to them.) Drain and squeeze out the juice, then blend the leaves to a paste in a food processor.

Add the cream and egg, and a little salt and pepper, and blend to a light homogenous cream.

Pour into a well-buttered, preferably non-stick, 20cm/8in mould or cake tin and bake for 30 minutes or until the top seems slightly firm. Turn out while still hot – it should come out easily.

VARIATION

For a quicker and equally delicious dish, fry 1 crushed garlic clove in 1 tbsp sunflower oil, add the washed spinach leaves, and when they soften, add double (heavy) cream, salt, pepper and a pinch of nutmeg.

500G/ 1 LB/ 2¹/₄ CUPS SMALL
WHITE HARICOT (NAVY) BEANS,
SOAKED IN WATER FOR 2 HOURS

1 MEDIUM CARROT, CUT INTO
4 SLICES

1 MEDIUM ONION, QUARTERED

A FEW CELERY LEAVES

2 GARLIC CLOVES, PEELED

2 MEDIUM TOMATOES, PEELED
AND CHOPPED

2 SPRIGS OF ROSEMARY

1 BAY LEAF

WHITE PEPPER

SALT

EXTRA VIRGIN OLIVE OIL

WHITE HARICOT (NAVY) BEAN POT

This is a good hot or cold accompaniment to egg dishes, flans and gratins, and fish. The vegetables and herbs lend a delicious flavour.

SERVES 6

Drain the beans and put them in a pot with the rest of the ingredients, except salt and oil. Cover with water and simmer for 1 hour or until tender, adding salt towards the end.

Drain and serve hot or cold with a drizzle of olive oil.

500G/ 1 LB (ABOUT 3–4 LARGISH)
COURGETTES (ZUCCHINI), CUT INTO
THIN SLICES

4 TBSP MILD EXTRA VIRGIN OLIVE
OIL OR SUNFLOWER OIL

1 GARLIC CLOVE, FINELY CHOPPED

SALT AND PEPPER

2 TSP DRIED MINT

JUICE OF ¹/₂ LEMON (OPTIONAL)

SAUTÉED COURGETTES (ZUCCHINI)

Courgettes (zucchini) sautéed in oil have a much better taste than boiled ones. These can be served hot, or cold with lemon juice.

SERVES 4–6

In a large frying pan, sauté the courgettes (zucchini) in the oil over medium heat with the garlic, season with salt and pepper and turn the slices over a few times, until they are tender.

Add the mint towards the end, and the lemon juice, if using.

LEFT *White Haricot
(Navy) Bean Pot*

1 GARLIC CLOVE, CRUSHED

4–5 TBSP EXTRA VIRGIN OLIVE OIL

8 FROZEN ARTICHOKE HEARTS OR BOTTOMS, DEFROSTED AND CUT INTO SLICES

4 MEDIUM-SIZED NEW POTATOES, BOILED, SKINNED AND SLICED

SALT AND PEPPER

SAUTÉED ARTICHOKE HEARTS AND POTATOES

This is easy to make with frozen artichokes (available from Middle Eastern Stores). It can be served as a first course.

SERVES 4

Fry the garlic in the oil over low heat for a few seconds, stirring. Add the artichokes and sauté, stirring, until tender. Add the potatoes, season with salt and pepper, and cook, stirring for a few minutes more until the potatoes are heated through. Serve hot.

400G/14 OZ OKRA, PREFERABLY YOUNG AND SMALL

1 MEDIUM ONION, CUT IN HALF AND SLICED

3 TBSP VEGETABLE OR LIGHT EXTRA VIRGIN OLIVE OIL

2 GARLIC CLOVES, CHOPPED

4 MEDIUM TOMATOES, PEELED AND CHOPPED

SALT AND PEPPER

JUICE OF 1/2 LEMON

1–2 TSP GRANULATED SUGAR, TO TASTE

A SMALL BUNCH (1/4 CUP) FLAT-LEAFED PARSLEY OR CORIANDER (CILANTRO), CHOPPED

RIGHT *Okra in Tomato Sauce*

OKRA IN TOMATO SAUCE

Okra is a vegetable much loved in the eastern Mediterranean. But, unlike the aubergine (eggplant), which the Turks claim to serve in a hundred different ways, *bamia* is almost always cooked with onions and tomatoes. It is served hot, with rice, or cold, as an appetizer.

SERVES 4

Trim the conical caps and wash and drain the okra.

Fry the onion in the oil over medium heat until golden. Add the garlic and stir for a moment or two.

Put in the okra and sauté for about 5 minutes, turning over the pods. Add the tomatoes, salt, pepper, lemon juice and sugar and cook for 15 minutes. Stir in the herbs before serving.

1 LARGE ONION, SLICED

3 TBSP GROUNDNUT
(PEANUT) OR VEGETABLE
OIL

500G/ 1 LB PUMPKIN,
CUT INTO 2 CM/ ³/4 IN
CUBES

SALT AND PLENTY OF
PEPPER

1 TSP GRANULATED
SUGAR, OR TO TASTE
(OPTIONAL)

1 TSP CINNAMON

3 TBSP RAISINS

3 TBSP PINE NUTS

SAUTÉED PUMPKIN WITH RAISINS AND PINE NUTS

**The raisin and pine nut partnership is
something the Arabs brought to the Mediterranean
region, all the way to Spain and Sicily. You
find the garnish with spinach, rice, bulgur and all
kinds of dishes. It goes well with pumpkin in
this North African dish, which provides a certain
delicate sweetness to a vegetarian meal.**

SERVES 4

In a large frying pan, fry the onion in the oil over
medium heat, stirring occasionally, until soft and golden.

Add the pumpkin and sauté over low heat for 5
minutes, turning the pieces over.

Add salt, pepper, sugar, cinnamon and raisins.
Cover with a tight-fitting lid and cook for about 20
minutes or until the pumpkin is tender, turning the
pumpkin over occasionally. It will release its own juices.

Dry-toast the pine nuts or fry them in just a film of
oil in a frying pan, shaking the pan to brown them lightly
all over.

Serve the pumpkin hot or cold, sprinkled with the
pine nuts.

FISH AND SEAFOOD

Much of Mediterranean fish cookery is a matter of grilling (broiling), frying, roasting or poaching, and marrying the fish with a dressing or sauce. Choose your fish and cook it by one of the methods on pages 150 to 163. Serve it with one of the marinades, dressings or sauces on pages 144 to 150. Popular Mediterranean fish include sea bass, sea bream, sole, gurnard, John Dory, red mullet, hake and tuna. Most of them are easy to obtain, but you can substitute fish from other seas, such as cod, haddock, halibut, snapper and catfish.

JUICE OF *1* LEMON

6 TBSP EXTRA VIRGIN OLIVE OIL

SALT AND PEPPER

3 TBSP FINELY CHOPPED FLAT-
LEAFED PARSLEY

OIL AND LEMON DRESSING

**This is the standard, all-purpose
Mediterranean dressing for fish.**

SERVES *4*

Mix the ingredients cold and pour over the fish.

*125*ML/*4* FL OZ/ *1/2* CUP LIGHT
EXTRA VIRGIN OLIVE OIL

JUICE OF *1/2* LEMON

4 MEDIUM TOMATOES, SKINNED
AND DICED

SALT AND PEPPER

1–1 1/2 TSP GRANULATED SUGAR

WARM LEMON AND TOMATO DRESSING

**This is particularly delicious with
grilled (broiled) fish.**

SERVES *4*

Simply put the oil, lemon juice, tomatoes, salt, pepper and sugar in a pan and heat through.

3 MEDIUM TOMATOES

1/2 –1 SMALL RED CHILLI

1 GARLIC CLOVE, CRUSHED

2.5 CM/*1* IN PIECE OF GINGER,
GRATED (OR USE THE JUICE,
PRESSED OUT USING A GARLIC
PRESS)

1/2 RED ONION, FINELY CHOPPED

JUICE OF *1/2* LIME OR LEMON

4 TBSP EXTRA VIRGIN OLIVE OIL

SALT AND PEPPER

1 TSP GRANULATED SUGAR

SAUCE VIERGE

**This spicy raw tomato sauce goes well with raw
marinated fish and with cold fish.**

SERVES *4*

Skin and finely chop the tomatoes, and finely chop the chilli. Mix with the rest of the ingredients to taste.

1 LARGE BUNCH (²/₃ CUP) CORIANDER (CILANTRO), CHOPPED

4 GARLIC CLOVES, CRUSHED

1 TSP GROUND CUMIN

1 TSP PAPRIKA

¼–½ TSP CHILLI POWDER (OPTIONAL)

6 TBSP GROUNDNUT (PEANUT) OR LIGHT EXTRA VIRGIN OLIVE OIL

JUICE OF 1 LEMON OR 3 TBSP WHITE WINE VINEGAR

CHERMOULA

This hot, spicy, garlicky mixture is the all-purpose, ubiquitous Moroccan sauce for fish. It goes on every kind of fish – fried, grilled (broiled), baked and stewed. Use half the quantity to marinate the fish for 30 minutes before cooking, and pour the rest on as a sauce before serving.

SERVES 4

Blend all the ingredients together in a food processor.

2 HEADS OF GARLIC, PREFERABLY YOUNG, WITH FAT CLOVES

250ML/8 FL OZ/1 CUP DRY WHITE WINE

2 TBSP EXTRA VIRGIN OLIVE OIL

SALT AND PEPPER

GARLIC PURÉE

Cooks in Provence have many ways of turning garlic into something mild and delicate. This *purée d'ail*, in which garlic is simmered in white wine, is delicious with all kinds of fish. I have tried it with pan-fried fillet of whiting and also with grilled (broiled) bream. Spread it on just before serving.

SERVES 4–6

Peel the garlic cloves and boil them in the wine for 15–20 minutes or until very soft. Drain and mash to a purée with a fork, then stir in the oil and a little salt and pepper.

A VERY LARGE BUNCH (2 CUPS)
FLAT-LEAFED PARSLEY, STEMS
REMOVED

75G/ 3 OZ/ 1/2 CUP PINE NUTS

5 SMALL GHERKINS

8 PITTED GREEN OLIVES

3 GARLIC CLOVES, CRUSHED

3 TBSP WHITE WINE VINEGAR OR
THE JUICE OF 1/2 LEMON

SALT AND PEPPER

ABOUT 250ML/ 8 FL OZ/ 1 CUP
LIGHT EXTRA VIRGIN OLIVE OIL

SALSA VERDE

**This Italian herb sauce is a good accompaniment to
marinated and cold poached fish. The sauce
keeps well in a jar with a layer of oil at the top.**

SERVES 6

Blend all the ingredients except the oil in a food processor, then add the oil gradually – enough to achieve a light paste.

---

1 SLICE OF WHITE BREAD, CRUSTS
REMOVED

175G/ 6 OZ/ 1 1/4 CUPS PINE NUTS

JUICE OF 1–2 LEMONS, TO TASTE

1–2 GARLIC CLOVES, CRUSHED

SALT AND WHITE PEPPER

120ML/ 3 1/2 FL OZ/ 1/2 CUP SESAME
OR VEGETABLE OIL

TARATOR

**This lemony pine nut sauce is often seen
on grand Arab buffet tables spread all over a large
skinned, boned and re-shaped poached
fish, but a dollop of it is equally good with a
piece of cold fish.**

SERVES 6

Soak the bread in water and squeeze dry. Put it in a food processor with the pine nuts, lemon juice and garlic, a little salt and pepper, and purée, adding enough oil to achieve a creamy mixture with the consistency of mayonnaise.

RIGHT *Halibut Poached in White Wine
(see page 160) with Salsa Verde*

2 RED (BELL) PEPPERS

500G/ 1 LB (ABOUT 6 MEDIUM) TOMATOES

1 LARGE SLICE OF WHITE BREAD, CRUSTS REMOVED

5 TBSP EXTRA VIRGIN OLIVE OIL

3 GARLIC CLOVES, CRUSHED

100G/ 3½ OZ/ ¾ CUP BLANCHED ALMONDS

JUICE OF ½ LEMON, OR MORE TO TASTE

½ RED CHILLI PEPPER

SALT AND PEPPER

VARIATION

Blanched hazelnuts or a mixture of almonds and hazelnuts can be used instead.

ROMESCO

I love this roast pepper and almond sauce.
It is an approximation of the famous Spanish sauce
based on the dark, wine-coloured *ñora* peppers,
which are sweet and slightly hot. The rich nutty,
piquant flavour makes it a delightful accompaniment
to vegetables as well as fish. It keeps well in a jar with
a film of olive oil at the top. Serve it with
grilled (broiled), steamed or fried fish and seafood,
and with fish stews and soups.

SERVES 12

Roast the peppers (see page 216) and tomatoes under the grill (broiler). Skin them and deseed the peppers.

Fry the bread in 2 tbsp of the oil over medium heat until golden, turning it over once. Add the garlic and stir until it just begins to colour.

Toast the almonds in a dry frying pan, shaking the pan to brown them all over.

In a food processor, blend the fried bread, garlic, almonds, the remaining oil, lemon juice and chilli to a paste. Add the peppers, tomatoes and salt and pepper, and blend to a creamy consistency.

Serve in a bowl and pass round for people to help themselves.

RIGHT *Grilled (Broiled) Tuna (see page 157) with Romesco*

250G/ ½ LB (2 MEDIUM) ONIONS, CUT IN HALF AND SLICED

2 TBSP EXTRA VIRGIN OLIVE OIL

2 BAY LEAVES

1 SPRIG OF THYME

1 SPRIG OF ROSEMARY

1 TBSP HONEY

1 TSP WHITE WINE VINEGAR

SALT AND PLENTY OF PEPPER

ONION FONDUE WITH HONEY

**Use this to accompany or to stuff a fish.
Because the fondue (the onions are melting
soft, hence the name) is sweet, it is
best to use a tart dressing of oil and lemon
on the fish to cut the sweetness.**

SERVES 4

In a covered pan, cook the onion in the oil with the bay leaves, thyme and rosemary over a very low heat for about 30 minutes, stirring occasionally, until the onion is very soft and just beginning to colour. It will stew in its juice rather than fry.

Add the honey, vinegar, salt and pepper and cook over medium heat for another 10 minutes or until much of the liquid has evaporated.

STUFFED FISH

SERVES 4

Ask the fishmonger to scale and clean a bream or sea bass weighing about 1.5 kg/3 lb and to remove the bones through the back. Or have the fish filleted with the head left on one of the fillets. Brush the fish with 2–3 tbsp extra virgin olive oil and season lightly inside and out with salt and pepper. Stuff with Onion Fondue with Honey or Garlic Purée (see page 145) and place in a baking dish. Pour on the juice of ½ lemon or about 4 tbsp dry white wine. Put under the grill (broiler) for 5–6 minutes until the skin is crisp and brown. Then bake in a pre-heated 190°C/375°F/Gas 5 oven for 20–25 minutes or until the flesh flakes easily away from the bone when you cut it with a pointed knife.

1 SEA BASS OR BREAM WEIGHING ABOUT 2.5KG/5LB

6 TBSP LIGHT EXTRA VIRGIN OLIVE OIL

SALT AND PEPPER

JUICE OF 1 LEMON

6 TBSP DRY WHITE WINE

VARIATION

For a Moroccan variation marinate the fish for 30 minutes in the following mixture, blended in a food processor: a bunch (½ cup) of coriander (cilantro), a bunch (½ cup) of flat-leafed parsley, 3 crushed garlic cloves, salt, 6 tbsp extra virgin olive oil, ½–1 tsp ground ginger, and ¼–½ tsp saffron powder.

ROAST FISH

Any large fish is suitable for this recipe. Sea bass is the grandest fish of the Mediterranean, but a large bream (daurade) is marvellous too.

SERVES 8

Pre-heat the oven to 190°C/375°F/Gas 5.

Brush the fish with 1–2 tbsp of the oil and season lightly inside and out with salt and pepper.

Place in a baking dish with a mixture of the lemon juice, the remaining oil and the white wine.

Put under the grill (broiler) for 5–6 minutes until the skin is crisp and brown, then bake for about 35 minutes or until the flesh begins to flake away from the bone when you cut it with a pointed knife.

152

RIGHT *Roast Bream Stuffed with Onion Fondue with Honey (page 150)*

2 SALMON FILLETS, TOGETHER
WEIGHING ABOUT 1 KG/2 LB, WITH
THE SKINS LEFT ON

3 TBSP COARSE SEA SALT

200ML/7 FL OZ/3/4 CUP LIGHT
EXTRA VIRGIN OLIVE OIL

JUICE OF 1 LEMON

A LARGE BUNCH (ABOUT 1/2 CUP)
OF MIXED HERBS INCLUDING
CHERVIL, CHIVES AND DILL,
CHOPPED

MARINATED FISH

**Fish lightly cured in salt and marinated in
olive oil, lemon juice and herbs is a tradition in
the Mediterranean. In the old days a variety
of fish were used. These days in France, salmon –
not a Mediterranean fish – has been
adopted as the popular one for this treatment.
Start the night before you plan to serve.
It is important to use very fresh fish.**

SERVES 10

Carefully remove any small bones from the fillets (tweezers will help). Sprinkle the fillets with the salt, on the skin side as well as inside.

Put the fillets together to re-form the fish and place in a large deep plate that can hold the liquid when it is drawn out. Cover with cling film (plastic wrap) and leave in the refrigerator for about 12 hours, turning the salmon over when the juices start to collect.

Scrape off the salt with a spatula and wipe the fish with paper towels, then rinse the fish in cold water under the tap. Taste a piece. If it is too salty, soak it in fresh water for as long as it takes to get rid of the saltiness. Mix together the oil, lemon juice and herbs and pour into the bottom of 1 or 2 large dishes. Lay the fillets, flesh side down, on this marinade and refrigerate, covered with cling film (plastic wrap) for about 3 hours.

Before serving, cut diagonal slices across the grain of the fish – they can be very thin or fairly thick.

VARIATIONS

The fish is also delicious marinated in the herbs and olive oil alone, with no lemon.

Serve with a sauce: Salsa Verde (see page 146); Aïoli (page 220); or Tarator (page 146). It is also lovely served with the raw tomato sauce, Sauce Vierge (page 144).

TIP

Do not use fine salt as it penetrates the fish and makes it too salty, instead of drawing out the juices.

Pan-cooked Fish Fillet

Cooking filleted fish in a large heavy pan or Spanish *plancha*, or on a thick metal sheet, barely filmed with oil, is currently the most popular way in France. It is also the easiest. The French call it *poêlé*. It is fashionable to cook the fillet on one side (the skin side) only. The result is a wonderfully moist, juicy texture. You can use any fish fillet, large or small, but it must have the skin on. Sea bass fillets and whole sides of salmon cook beautifully in this way. Scoring the thick part on the skin side prevents curling and allows the fish to cook evenly.

Oil the pan or sheet and heat it to just below smoking point. Brush the fish with oil and sprinkle with salt. Place it, skin side down, in the pan, and cook, uncovered, over a medium heat. It will gradually cook through to the top. The fish is done when it becomes opaque right through and the flesh flakes easily. When cooking a thin fillet, the heat can be quite fierce. A thick piece is best done over a gentle heat. A fat salmon fillet can take more than 20 minutes. Some people like to finish by putting the fish, brushed with oil, under the grill (broiler) for a few seconds.

If you do not have a very large frying pan or *plancha*, cut the fillets into manageable pieces (escalopes).

Serve sprinkled with parsley and accompanied with a sauce such as Salsa Verde (see page 146), Romesco (page 148), Aïoli (page 220), Tarator (page 146), Sauce Vierge (page 144) or Onion Fondue with Honey (page 150).

GRILLED (BROILED) FISH

**Cooking fish over charcoal is an old and enchanting way of doing
things in the Mediterranean.**

For fish steaks, use tuna (currently very fashionable), swordfish, hake, turbot, cod,
haddock or halibut. Simply brush the fish with olive oil and sprinkle with salt and
pepper. Place about 5cm/2in from the fire, on a well oiled grill over glowing embers, or
under the oven grill (broiler). Cook for 2–4 minutes on each side. The fish is cooked
when the flesh flakes away from the bone when you cut with the point of a knife. It is
important not to overcook. The best way to cook tuna is to sear it on the outside at high
heat (close to the fire) and to leave it underdone inside.

For whole fish, use small or medium-sized bream, gurnard, red mullet, sardines
and also flat fish such as sole and skate. Have them scaled and cleaned but keep the
heads on. Brush with extra virgin oil and season with salt and pepper. Cook for 2–5
minutes on each side, depending on the size. Cut into one fish with a pointed knife to
see if they are done.

For fish fillet (large fish split along the backbone), use sea bass, bream, hake,
swordfish, turbot, salmon. Leave the skin on. Brush with extra virgin olive oil and season
with salt and pepper. Cook on the skin side only, not too close to the fire, and do not turn
over or the fish will dry out. It does cook through.

Serve grilled fish with a dressing or sauce. Dress with Oil and Lemon dressing (see
page 144), adding, if desired, chopped herbs such as fennel, thyme, marjoram, oregano,
or tarragon, or try Warm Lemon and Tomato Dressing (see page 144). Accompany with
any of the sauces featured between pages 144 and 150 and lemon wedges.

DEEP-FRIED FISH

Deep-frying is the most popular way of cooking fish in the Arab world. The method was introduced by the Arabs in the early Middle Ages to Spain and Sicily. Southern Italians excel at their *fritti misti* – a medley that may include red mullet, sardines, anchovies, whitebait, fillet of sole, baby hake, baby squid and large prawns (shrimp). The Andalusians are the world's best at frying any kind of fish and seafood. Many people these days are averse to this method of cooking, but the result is delightful and worth trying.

To ensure success you must follow these rules:

- Use olive oil to fry because it can reach high temperatures without deteriorating (it can be filtered and re-used). There must be enough oil to cover the fish and the temperature should remain constant. Always start frying at high heat to seal the fish, then turn the heat down to moderate if necessary.

- Use a large, deep pan so that there is no risk of the oil bubbling over.

- Fry fish of about the same size together.

- Season the fish with salt inside and out and cover entirely, but lightly, with flour.

- Small fish must be fried very briefly at a very high heat so that they are crisp and brown but still moist inside.

- Larger fish take longer (3–4 minutes on each side) and need a lower temperature so they have time to cook inside before the skin gets burnt.

- Fish steaks or fillets are best first dipped in seasoned flour then in lightly beaten egg for extra protection.

- When frying, turn only once, lift out and drain on paper towels.

- Prawns (shrimp), squid and fat mussels are usually dipped in batter before frying. To make a batter for 500g/1lb seafood to serve 4 people, mix 120g/4oz/1 cup flour with 1 tsp baking powder, ½ tsp salt, 2 tbsp olive oil and 150ml/5fl oz/⅔ cup water. Beat well and let it rest for 30 minutes.

150ML/5 FL OZ/ 2/3 CUP DRY
WHITE WINE

150ML/5 FL OZ/ 2/3 CUP WATER

2 BAY LEAVES

A FEW PARSLEY STALKS

A LITTLE SALT AND WHITE PEPPER

A PINCH OF SAFFRON (OPTIONAL)

4 FISH STEAKS OR FILLETS

VARIATION

This is a simple and
marvellous Italian way with
fish: fry 1 chopped garlic
clove in 4 tbsp extra virgin
olive oil over low heat. Add
150ml/5fl oz/ 2/3 cup dry
white wine and 2 chopped
tomatoes. Bring to the boil
and add the fish fillets.
Simmer for 5 minutes.
Add 1 tbsp chopped flat-
leafed parsley and serve in
a soup bowl with some of
the liquid.

POACHED FISH IN WHITE WINE

**Poached fish – fillets or steaks – are good to
serve hot or cold. You may use any white fish.
The saffron is a Mediterranean touch which you
occasionally find in various countries.**

SERVES 4

Put all the ingredients except the fish in a pan wide
enough to contain the fish in one layer. Bring to the boil
and lower the heat to a simmer.

Add the fish and simmer gently for 3–6 minutes,
depending on the thickness and type of fish, until the
flesh is opaque and flakes when you cut into it with the
point of a knife.

Serve with Oil and Lemon Dressing (see page 144).

Accompany with Salsa Verde (page 146), Sauce
Vierge (page 144), Garlic Purée (page 145), Mayonnaise
or Aïoli (page 220), or Tarator (page 146).

4 *FISH FILLETS*

25G/ 1 OZ/ 2 *TBSP BUTTER*

1 *TBSP SUNFLOWER OR VEGETABLE OIL*

SALT AND PEPPER

AROMATICS (SEE BELOW)

SAUTÉED FISH

**This is a quick and easy way to cook fish fillets.
Another advantage is that you
can incorporate herbs and aromatics.**

SERVES 4

Sauté the fish in a mixture of sizzling butter and oil, adding salt and pepper and aromatics, for about 5 minutes or until the fish turns opaque and begins to flake. Turn the fillets over once.

AROMATICS

For a Moroccan flavour, add ⅓ tsp powdered ginger and ¼ tsp saffron to the pan with the butter and oil.

For another North African flavour, add 1 tsp ground cumin, 1 tsp paprika, ¼ tsp cayenne, the juice of ½ lemon and a good bunch (½ cup) chopped coriander (cilantro).

For a touch of southern France, add 2–3 tbsp chopped fennel leaves and 1 tbsp Pastis.

For another Moroccan variation, add ½–1 Preserved Lemon Peel (see page 219), rinsed and cut into small pieces, 8–12 green olives (pitted if preferred) and 2 tbsp capers.

2 x 500g/ 1 lb PACKETS
OF BOUGHT FROZEN PUFF
PASTRY, DEFROSTED

1 EGG, SIZE 1 (U.S. LARGE),
SEPARATED

2.5kg/5 lb SALMON OR
SEA BASS

3 TBSP SUNFLOWER OR
VEGETABLE OIL

JUICE OF 1/2 LEMON

SALT AND WHITE PEPPER

FISH COOKED IN PASTRY

**This is a Mediterranean version
of a *poisson en croûte*. Salmon and sea bass are
both suitable; ask the fishmonger to fillet
and skin the fish for you.**

SERVES 8–10

Pre-heat the oven to 230°C/450°F/Gas 8.

The pastry packets are divided into two pieces of
dough, each weighing 250g/8oz. Stick two pieces from
one packet together and roll out into a long, thin piece,
about the thickness of a coin. Cut out in the shape of the
filleted fish but slightly larger, adding a tail. Save any
leftover pastry for decoration.

Lay the fish shape on a damp baking sheet and
leave it in a cold place to rest for 15 minutes. Brush it
with egg white to prevent it from getting too soggy with
the fish juices, and prick it all over with a fork so that it
does not puff up unevenly.

Bake it for 8 minutes or until crisp and lightly
coloured. Turn it over, brush the other side with egg
white, put it back in the oven and bake for a few more
minutes until this side is golden. Let it cool.

Brush the fish fillets with the oil and lemon juice
and season with salt and pepper. Place them on top of
each other on the baked pastry.

Roll out the remaining pieces of dough, sticking
them together to make one large sheet, the thickness of
a coin, that will cover the fish.

Cover the fish entirely with the dough, and cut round it, leaving a margin of about 2.5cm/1in, including around the tail.

Using a rounded knife, lift the edge of the baked pastry base and tuck the dough margin underneath, pressing gently to seal.

Decorate the pastry. Using a teaspoon, make a scale design on the body. Using the leftover scraps of dough, attach thin ribbons to represent the tail, gills and fins and stick on a little ball for the eye.

Brush all over with egg yolk and bake for 15 minutes until puffed up and golden. Then lower the heat to 150°C/300°F/Gas 2 and bake for another 30 minutes.

If the pastry seems to brown too quickly, cover it with foil or with slightly dampened greaseproof (parchment) paper.

Serve accompanied with Fresh Tomato Sauce (see page 218), adding the ginger, or with Warm Lemon and Tomato Dressing (see page 144).

4 RED MULLET, WEIGHING ABOUT
1 KG/2 LB IN TOTAL, SCALED AND
CLEANED BUT WITH THE HEADS
LEFT ON

4 GARLIC CLOVES, CHOPPED

4 TBSP LIGHT EXTRA VIRGIN
OLIVE OIL

500G/1 LB (ABOUT 6) RIPE
TOMATOES, PEELED AND CHOPPED

SALT AND PEPPER

1 1/2 TSP GRANULATED SUGAR

4 LEMON SLICES

12 BLACK OLIVES, PITTED
(OPTIONAL)

3 TBSP CHOPPED FLAT-LEAFED
PARSLEY

RED MULLET
IN TOMATO SAUCE

This dish looks beautiful, red on red.

SERVES 4

In a large frying pan that can hold the fish in one layer, fry the garlic in the oil over low heat until it just begins to colour. Add the tomatoes, salt, pepper, sugar and the lemon slices and simmer for 10 minutes, then put in the fish and the olives, if using, and simmer for 4 minutes or until the fish flakes easily away from the bone. Add the parsley before serving.

1 LITRE/ 1 3/4 PINTS/ 4 1/2 CUPS MILK

1 1/2 TBSP TOMATO PURÉE (PASTE)

1/4 TSP SAFFRON

8 EGGS, SIZE 1 (U.S. LARGE)

SALT AND WHITE PEPPER

BUTTER, FOR GREASING

750G/ 1 1/2 LB POTATOES, PEELED
AND SLICED

1.5KG/ 3 LB FISH FILLETS, CUT
INTO 4 CM/ 1 3/4 IN PIECES

FOR THE SAUCE

4–5 GARLIC CLOVES

1/2 –1 RED CHILLI PEPPER, FINELY
CHOPPED OR A GOOD PINCH OF
CAYENNE

2 TBSP OLIVE OIL

2 x 400G/ 14 OZ TINS ITALIAN
CHOPPED TOMATOES

SALT

1–2 TSP GRANULATED SUGAR

CREAMY FISH FLAN WITH SPICY TOMATO SAUCE

**This fish dish – a delicately flavoured creamy
flan, served with a hot peppery sauce –
is from Provence. It is the kind
of dish you can easily make for a lot of people.
You may use one type of fish
only or a variety of firm white fish such
as cod and haddock, as well as salmon. Buy fish
fillets and have them skinned.**

SERVES 8 OR MORE

Pre-heat the oven to 180°C/350°F/Gas 4.

In a saucepan over medium heat, bring the milk to the boil. Dilute the tomato purée (paste) with a little of the milk and add it to the pan along with the saffron.

Beat the eggs in a bowl then gradually beat in the hot milk. Add salt and pepper to taste.

Grease a 36cm/14in baking dish with butter. Arrange a layer of potatoes at the bottom, then add a layer of fish, sprinkling lightly with salt. Pour the milk and egg mixture over the top.

Place the dish in an oven tray and pour water into the tray up to the level of the custard so that the flan cooks *au bain-marie*. Bake for 1–1¼ hours or until the custard sets.

Meanwhile make the sauce. Fry the garlic with the chilli pepper in the oil until the aroma rises. Add the tomatoes, salt and sugar and cook for 10 minutes.

Serve the flan hot, accompanied with the sauce.

FOR THE COUSCOUS

FOR THE COUSCOUS

500G/ 1 LB/ 2½ CUPS COUSCOUS

600ML/ 20 FL OZ/ 2½ CUPS WARM WATER

½–1 TSP SALT

3–4 TBSP GROUNDNUT (PEANUT) OIL OR LIGHT VEGETABLE OIL

FOR THE FISH

4–5 GARLIC CLOVES, CHOPPED

3 TBSP GROUNDNUT (PEANUT) OR VEGETABLE OIL

1 KG/ 2 LB PLUM TOMATOES, PEELED AND CHOPPED

SALT

2 TSP GRANULATED SUGAR

1–2 CHILLIES, CUT OPEN AND DESEEDED

2.5 CM/ 1 IN PIECE OF GINGER, PEELED AND CUT INTO SMALL PIECES

750G/ 1½ LB (2 LARGE) QUINCES

1 KG/ 2 LB FISH FILLET, SKINNED

TIP

Quinces are a very hard fruit and you will need a large strong knife to cut them.

FISH COUSCOUS WITH QUINCE

This delicious Moroccan-inspired couscous is best made with skinned fillets of a firm white fish such as cod, haddock or whiting.

SERVES 8

Pre-heat the oven to 200°C/400°F/Gas 6.

Soak and prepare the couscous in a baking dish according to the directions on pages 93–4, cover with foil and set aside.

Fry the garlic in the oil until it just begins to colour. Add the tomatoes, salt, sugar and chillies. Crush the ginger pieces in a garlic press over the pan to extract the juice, discarding the pressed ginger. Simmer over low heat. Peel, core and slice the quinces and add them to the pan immediately, before they turn brown.

Cook, covered, for 15–30 minutes or until the quinces are tender. The time varies depending on the size, quality and ripeness of the fruit. Remove one or both of the chillies when you think the sauce is spicy enough.

About 20 minutes before serving, put the couscous, still covered with foil, in the oven to heat through.

About 5–10 minutes before serving add the fish to the sauce and simmer until the flesh begins to flake. Bring the fish stew and couscous to the table in separate serving dishes. Serve in soup plates, the couscous first and the stew on top.

4 GARLIC CLOVES, CRUSHED

1 1/2 TSP GROUND CUMIN

SALT

ABOUT 100ML/ 3 1/2 FL OZ/ 1/2 CUP
OLIVE OIL

4 SMALL WINGS OF SKATE
WEIGHING 1 KG/ 2 LB IN TOTAL

500G/ 1 LB (ABOUT 4–5) NEW
POTATOES, BOILED AND SLICED

PEPPER

2 TBSP CAPERS

1 LEMON, QUARTERED

VARIATION

Pieces of skate from a
large fish can be used but
they must first be boiled
for about 10 minutes.

SKATE WITH CUMIN
AND POTATOES

**All over North Africa, cumin is the
standard flavouring for fish. Small skate, tender
enough to fry quickly, should be used
for this Tunisian dish. The wings are bought
already dressed from the fishmonger.**

SERVES 4

Mix together the garlic, cumin, salt, and 3–4 tbsp of
the oil. Cut the fish into pieces, about 5cm/2in wide,
cutting in between the long soft bones, and rub the
pieces with the garlic mixture.

In a large frying pan, fry the fish pieces in batches
in shallow oil, giving them about 4 minutes on each side,
until the flesh begins to flake away from the bone.
Transfer to a baking dish, cover with foil and keep warm
in the oven.

Sauté the potatoes slowly in the same oil, adding
salt and pepper and more oil, and turning them over
until they are lightly golden. Add the capers towards
the end.

Serve the fish hot on a bed of the sautéed potatoes,
with lemon wedges.

2 GARLIC CLOVES, CHOPPED

125G/ 4¹/₂ OZ PEELED COOKED KING PRAWNS (SHRIMP) OR ABOUT 10 GREY PRAWNS (UNCOOKED SHRIMP)

2 TBSP OLIVE OIL

SALT AND PEPPER

1¹/₂ TSP TOMATO PURÉE (PASTE)

3 TBSP COGNAC

SAUTÉED PRAWNS (SHRIMP) WITH COGNAC

Cooked king prawns (shrimp) are common in supermarkets now, but if you can get hold of grey (uncooked) frozen ones, they are even better. This makes a luxurious dish for two. Large uncooked prawns need shelling and deveining. To do this, remove the black thread that runs the length of the prawn with a sharp knife.

SERVES 2

Sauté the garlic and the prawns (shrimp) for 30 seconds in the oil, stirring, until the pre-cooked prawns are heated through or until the uncooked ones turn pink. Add salt and pepper, the tomato purée (paste) and cognac and cook for a further 30 seconds. To serve, you can ignite the sauce and flambée it, if you wish.

2KG/ 4¹/₂ LB MUSSELS

2 GARLIC CLOVES, FINELY
CHOPPED OR CRUSHED

2 TBSP EXTRA VIRGIN OLIVE OIL

500ML/ 18 FL OZ/ 2¹/₄ CUPS
DRY WHITE WINE

BLACK PEPPER

A HANDFUL OF FLAT-LEAFED
PARSLEY, CHOPPED

MUSSELS WITH GARLIC AND WHITE WINE

Fashionable Belgian mussels-and-chips restaurants in Paris serve mussels in thirty different ways, but the classic and simple *moules à la marinière* is how people still choose to make them at home in the south of France.

SERVES 4–6

Prepare the mussels (see page 216).

In a very large pan, fry the garlic in the oil until it just begins to colour. Add the white wine and boil for 5 minutes.

Add the mussels and plenty of pepper. Cover the pan and cook over low heat for about 2 minutes – until the mussels open. Immediately remove from the heat.

Discard the mussels that did not open. Use a slotted spoon to transfer the mussels to serving bowls or soup plates. Strain the winey mussel broth through a thin muslin (cheesecloth) or fine strainer and pour a little into each bowl. Sprinkle with parsley.

500G/ 1 LB SMALL SQUID

2 GARLIC CLOVES, CHOPPED

1 RED CHILLI, SEEDED AND
VERY FINELY CHOPPED

3 TBSP OLIVE OIL

SALT AND PEPPER

1 TBSP LEMON JUICE

1 TBSP CHOPPED FLAT-LEAFED
PARSLEY

1 LEMON, CUT IN WEDGES

BABY SQUID WITH GARLIC AND CHILLIES

SERVES 4

Clean the squid and cut the body pouches into rings (see page 216).

Sauté the garlic and chilli pepper lightly in the oil over low heat.

When the garlic begins to colour, add the squid. Season with salt and pepper and sauté briefly over medium heat, turning over the pieces, for 2–3 minutes only. Sprinkle with lemon juice and parsley and serve at once, accompanied with the lemon wedges.

3 GARLIC CLOVES, FINELY CHOPPED

3 TBSP EXTRA VIRGIN OLIVE OIL

1 HOT RED CHILLI, SEEDED AND FINELY CHOPPED OR A VERY GOOD PINCH OF CHILLI POWDER (OPTIONAL)

500G/1 LB (6 MEDIUM) RIPE TOMATOES, PEELED AND CHOPPED

250ML/8 FL OZ/1 CUP DRY WHITE WINE

SALT AND PEPPER

1–2 TSP GRANULATED SUGAR OR TO TASTE

400G/14 OZ SPAGHETTINI, TAGLIOLINI OR TAGLIATELLE

500G/1 LB FLESHY SHELLED COOKED TIGER PRAWNS (SHRIMP)

4 TBSP FINELY CHOPPED FLAT-LEAFED PARSLEY

VARIATIONS

Make the sauce without tomatoes and add about 170ml/6fl oz/¾ cup double (heavy) cream at the end.

For a mixed seafood pasta use 750g/1½lb mussels and 250g/9oz small squid, cleaned and cut into rings (see page 216) with 200g/7oz prawns (shrimp).

PASTA WITH PRAWNS (SHRIMP)

Some years ago the *Sunday Telegraph* asked me to do a piece on the favourite dishes of famous Italians. I had to call Luciano Pavarotti, Claudio Abbado, Armani, Valentino and other personalities – chasing them around the world. Most of them said that their favourite food was the seafood pasta they made themselves. One or two used unorthodox ingredients such as champagne or a little curry and cream, but most were purists, preferring the classic dishes with prawns (shrimp) or mussels. This pasta can also be made with mixed seafood.

SERVES 4

Fry the garlic in the oil until it just begins to colour. Add the chilli and tomatoes, and cook for 5 minutes.

Add the wine. Season with salt and pepper, add sugar and simmer for 10 minutes to reduce.

Cook the pasta in plenty of boiling salted water until *al dente*.

Add the prawns (shrimp) to the sauce and heat through when the pasta is ready, and stir in the parsley.

Pour the sauce over the pasta and serve.

1 KG/ 2 LB MUSSELS

170ML/ 6 FL OZ/ 3/4 CUP DRY WHITE WINE

400G/ 14 OZ SPAGHETTI OR LINGUINE

SALT

2–4 GARLIC CLOVES, CHOPPED

6–8 TBSP EXTRA VIRGIN OLIVE OIL

BLACK PEPPER

5 TBSP CHOPPED FLAT-LEAFED PARSLEY

SPAGHETTI WITH MUSSELS IN WHITE WINE

Clams are often used rather than mussels, but mussels make sense because they are more fleshy. Here they are *in bianco*, that is, without tomatoes, which best preserves the pure flavour of the sea. Linguine may be used instead of spaghetti. Do not serve grated cheese – Parmesan or other – with this dish.

SERVES 4

Clean and prepare the mussels (see page 216). Put them in a large pan, with about half the wine. Cover and cook over a high heat for about 1 minute. Take the pan off the heat as soon as the mussels open. Discard any that remain closed. Strain the juices from the pan and reserve.

Cook the spaghetti in plenty of vigorously boiling salted water until *al dente*.

Meanwhile, heat the garlic in 1 tbsp of the oil over low heat until it begins to colour and the aroma rises. Add the strained mussel juice and the rest of the wine and oil and boil vigorously for a few minutes to reduce. Add pepper.

Drain the spaghetti as soon as it is *al dente*. Mix well with the sauce, sprinkle with pepper and plenty of parsley and serve with the mussels on top. Or you may mix the drained spaghetti in the pan with the mussels before serving.

8 SCALLOPS

1 TBSP LIGHT VEGETABLE OR EXTRA
VIRGIN OLIVE OIL

1/2 QUANTITY MIXED GREEN LEAF
AND HERB SALAD (PAGE 16)

FOR THE DRESSING

6 TBSP LIGHT EXTRA VIRGIN
OLIVE OIL

2 TBSP BALSAMIC VINEGAR

SALT AND PEPPER

SCALLOPS WITH BALSAMIC VINEGAR DRESSING

The secret of cooking scallops is to cook them as briefly as possible. They make a royal first course, served on a bed of Mixed Green Leaf and Herb Salad (see page 16), using the dressing in this recipe.

SERVES 2

Combine the dressing ingredients and use half the mixture to dress the green salad.

Wash the scallops and pull away the intestinal thread. Cook them in a greased frying pan for 30–40 seconds on each side. Serve hot on a bed of the dressed salad with a drizzle of dressing on each.

RIGHT *Scallops with Balsamic
Vinegar Dressing*

500G/1 LB (ABOUT 5) NEW
POTATOES

SALT AND PEPPER

500G/1 LB FIRM WHITE FISH
FILLET, SUCH AS COD, HADDOCK OR
MONKFISH

2 TBSP WHITE WINE VINEGAR

6 TBSP LIGHT EXTRA VIRGIN
OLIVE OIL

1 MILD ONION, RED OR WHITE,
FINELY CHOPPED

2 TBSP CAPERS

A GOOD BUNCH (1/2 CUP)
CORIANDER (CILANTRO), CHOPPED

MOROCCAN FISH SALAD

SERVES 4

Boil the potatoes in salted water until tender, then drain, peel and cut into 2.5cm/1in pieces.

Poach the fish in boiling salted water for 5 minutes or until it just begins to flake when you cut it with a knife. Let it cool and flake it into similar sized pieces.

Beat the vinegar and oil with a little salt and pepper and pour over the fish and potatoes in a serving bowl. Add the rest of the ingredients and mix gently. Allow to cool before serving.

250G/ 9 OZ/ 1 1/4 CUPS AMERICAN LONG-GRAIN RICE

SALT

4–6 TBSP LIGHT EXTRA VIRGIN OLIVE OIL

JUICE OF 1 LEMON OR TO TASTE

PEPPER

5 SPRING ONIONS (SCALLIONS), FINELY CHOPPED

A LARGE BUNCH (1/2 CUP) FLAT-LEAFED PARSLEY OR A MIXTURE OF HERBS, SUCH AS CHIVES, MINT AND CORIANDER (CILANTRO), CHOPPED

ABOUT 500G/ 1 LB POACHED FISH OR SEAFOOD, SUCH AS WHITE FISH, SQUID, PRAWNS (SHRIMP) AND MUSSELS

VARIATION

A ring of cold Tomato Risotto (see page 87) filled with a variety of poached seafood dressed with Oil and Lemon Dressing (see page 144) or with (cold) Lemon and Tomato Dressing (see page 144) is a spectacular variation.

SEAFOOD AND RICE SALAD

Made in large quantities, this is an ideal dish for a party. It is relatively cheap, beautiful to look at, can be prepared in advance, and tastes delicious. The seafood may include a firm-fleshed white fish, cut into pieces and poached; squid cut into rings and poached; peeled cooked prawns (shrimp); and mussels, in or out of their shells. (For preparing mussels and squid see page 216.)

SERVES 4

Cook the rice in boiling salted water for about 18 minutes until just tender, then drain.

Dress while still warm with the oil, lemon juice, salt and pepper. Let it cool and mix with the spring onions (scallions) and parsley or mixed herbs. Fold in the poached seafood.

Serve cold. You may like to accompany with Mayonnaise or Aïoli (see page 220) but it is not essential.

FOR THE SOAKED BREAD BASE

4 SLICES COUNTRY BREAD, ABOUT 1.25CM/1/2 IN THICK

175ML/6 FL OZ/3/4 CUP TOMATO JUICE

5 TBSP OLIVE OIL

2 TBSP RED OR WHITE WINE VINEGAR

SALT AND PEPPER

1/2–1 TSP HARISSA (OPTIONAL) (SEE PAGE 219)

FOR THE SALAD TOPPING

2 GREEN OR RED (BELL) PEPPERS

3 MEDIUM RIPE TOMATOES

1 x 200G/7 OZ TIN OF TUNA, DRAINED AND FLAKED

3 HARD-BOILED EGGS, QUARTERED

4–8 BLACK OLIVES

1–2 TBSP CAPERS, SQUEEZED OF THEIR VINEGAR (OPTIONAL)

1 x 50G TIN OF ANCHOVIES, DRAINED (OPTIONAL)

3–4 TBSP EXTRA VIRGIN OLIVE OIL

JUICE OF 1/2 LEMON

SALT AND PEPPER

ROAST (BELL) PEPPER, TOMATO, TUNA AND BREAD SALAD

Tunisia's famous salad *meshweya* (it means 'grilled') becomes a hearty summer's day meal when it is served on a bed of bread soaked with tomato juice and vinaigrette. Use a white rustic or country loaf. Adding Harissa is traditional, but I prefer this simple dish without.

SERVES 4

Cut the crusts off the bread and toast it. Arrange the slices side by side in a 23cm/9in wide shallow bowl.

Mix the tomato juice, olive oil, vinegar, salt and pepper, and Harissa, if using (I prefer it without), and pour over the bread so that it is thoroughly soaked.

To make the salad topping, place the peppers and tomatoes on a baking tray under the grill (broiler), turning them occasionally, or cook them on the barbecue.

Take the tomatoes out as soon as their skins come off easily. Peel and cut them into quarters. Take the peppers out when their skin is blackened in parts and blistered. Skin them, following the directions given on pages 216–7, and cut them into ribbons about 1.25cm/1/2in wide.

Arrange the elements of the salad – the (bell) peppers, tomatoes, flaked tuna, eggs, olives, capers and anchovies – on the soaked bread in a decorative way.

Mix the oil, lemon juice, salt and pepper and drizzle over the top.

1 BOTTLE (750ML/ 1¼ PINTS/ 3½ CUPS) DRY WHITE WINE

1.5 LITRES/ 2½ PINTS/ 7 CUPS WATER OR FISH STOCK (YOU MAY USE STOCK (BOUILLON) CUBES)

2 FRESH RED CHILLIES, DE-SEEDED

5 GARLIC CLOVES, SLIVERED

1 KG/ 2 LB NEW POTATOES

1 KG/ 2 LB PLUM TOMATOES, PEELED AND CUT IN HALF, OR 2 X 400G/ 14 OZ TINS PEELED PLUM TOMATOES

4 BAY LEAVES

A FEW PARSLEY STALKS

SALT TO TASTE

5 TBSP OLIVE OIL

1.5–2 KG/ 3–4½ LB FISH FILLETS

500G/ 1 LB SHELLED KING SIZE PRAWNS (SHRIMP) (OPTIONAL)

6 SCALLOPS (OPTIONAL)

1 KG/ 2 LB MUSSELS, CLEANED AND STEAMED OPEN (SEE PAGE 216) (OPTIONAL)

ITALIAN FISH SOUP

This is a dish for a party. I have made it with whole fish – bream, gurnard, red snapper, whiting and red mullet – which looks dramatic but is difficult to serve and there is the problem of bones to deal with. It is far easier to use fish fillets, such as monkfish, cod, turbot and red mullet. You can make it with fish fillets alone or you may add prawns (shrimp) and scallops or mussels.

SERVES 6–8

Put the wine and water or fish stock in a large pan. Add the chillies, garlic, potatoes, tomatoes, bay leaves, parsley stalks, and salt and bring to the boil. Simmer for 20 minutes.

Add the oil and the fish fillets and cook 5–10 minutes until they just begin to flake when you cut into them with a pointed knife. Add the prawns (shrimp), scallops and the mussels in their shells, if using, and cook for a further 30 seconds.

Serve in soup bowls with toasted bread rubbed with garlic. You may put the bread at the bottom of each soup bowl to soak up the broth.

500G/ 1 LB POTATOES, CUT INTO
THICK SLICES

2 MEDIUM TOMATOES, PEELED
AND QUARTERED

1 LITRE/ 1 ¾ PINTS/ 4 ½ CUPS
WATER

½ TSP PAPRIKA

¼ TSP HARISSA (SEE PAGE 216)
(OR MORE TO TASTE) OR A GOOD
PINCH OF CHILLI PEPPER

½ TSP CUMIN

3 GARLIC CLOVES, CHOPPED

JUICE OF ½ LEMON

SALT

3 TBSP EXTRA VIRGIN OLIVE OIL

500G/ 1 LB WHITE FISH FILLETS,
SKINNED

A LARGE BUNCH (½ CUP) FLAT-
LEAFED PARSLEY OR CORIANDER
(CILANTRO), FINELY CHOPPED

3–4 SPRIGS OF MINT, FINELY
CHOPPED

TUNISIAN FISH SOUP WITH POTATOES

There are fish soups with potatoes
and tomatoes in all the countries around the
Mediterranean. What is different in each
area is the type of fish used and the aromatics.
This simple version is a meal in itself.
Its appeal is the herby and peppery aromatics.
Start with only a little Harissa (see
page 216) or chilli pepper and add more later,
if you wish. I prefer it not too peppery.
Hake is often used in Tunisia for this soup,
but you can use any firm white fish such as
cod, haddock or turbot.

SERVES 4

Put all the ingredients except the oil, fish and herbs together in a pan. Simmer for 25 minutes or until the potatoes are tender.

Stir in the oil and add the fish. Cook another 10 minutes. Then gently break up the fillets into smaller pieces and add the herbs.

Serve hot with toasted bread.

25G/ 1 OZ/ 2 TBSP BUTTER

1 TBSP SUNFLOWER OR LIGHT
VEGETABLE OIL

1 MEDIUM ONION, CHOPPED

3 GARLIC CLOVES, FINELY CHOPPED

1 MEDIUM LEEK, SLICED

1 CELERY STICK, SLICED

250ML/ 8 FL OZ/ 1 CUP DRY
WHITE WINE

500ML/ 18 FL OZ/ 2 1/4 CUPS WATER

SALT AND WHITE PEPPER

A 7 CM/ 3 IN STRIP OF ORANGE PEEL

200G/ 7 OZ/ 1 MEDIUM–LARGE
POTATO, CUBED

1/2 TSP SAFFRON THREADS

600G/ 1 1/4 LB SKINNED FISH FILLET

150ML/ 5 FL OZ/ 2/3 CUP DOUBLE
(HEAVY) CREAM

VARIATION

Replace about 200g/7oz of
the fish with cooked prawns
(shrimp). Add them to
the pan just before you add
the cream.

FISH SOUP WITH SAFFRON AND CREAM

**This delicate creamy soup with the flavours
of the south of France is one of our
family favourites. It is extremely easy to make
with boneless fish fillet such as cod,
haddock, whiting or other white (non-oily) fish,
or, if you like, with a mixture of fish
and cooked prawns (shrimp). Serve it with
warmed or lightly toasted bread.**

SERVES 4

Heat the butter and oil in a large saucepan. Add the onion, garlic, leek and celery and sauté lightly until they are soft and beginning to colour slightly.

Pour in the white wine and water. Season with a little salt and pepper and add the orange peel. Simmer for 10 minutes.

Add the potatoes and cook for 20 minutes, adding water if necessary as the liquid evaporates. Add the saffron and fish fillets and cook for 8–10 minutes or until the fish turns opaque. Cut the fish into pieces.

Remove the orange peel, stir in the cream and cook for 1–2 minutes. Serve hot.

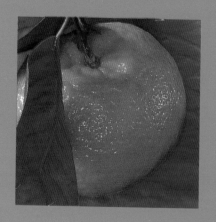

DESSERTS

The usual Mediterranean way to end a meal is with fruit: figs, grapes, apricots, dates, melons and watermelons, peaches, plums, cherries, apples, pears or oranges. Simply bring a bowl to the table, or peel and cut up a selection and arrange it on a platter. Another tradition is to offer dried fruit and nuts with coffee. Most of the desserts in this chapter are made with fruit to celebrate the Mediterranean's rich bounty. I have provided quite a few recipes – because I love desserts, and because they are all-important at dinner parties.

*A VARIETY OF FRUIT (ABOUT 1 KG/
2 LB), PEELED IF NECESSARY*

*4 TBSP GRANULATED SUGAR,
OR TO TASTE*

JUICE OF 1/2 – 1 LEMON

MACERATED FRUIT SALAD

**Leaving the fruit to macerate in a
mixture of lemon and sugar releases their
juices and gives them a richer, more
intense flavour. Use a good variety of fruit,
such as bananas, oranges, apples,
pears, apricots, strawberries, raspberries,
blueberries, seedless grapes,
kiwis, cherries, mangoes and pineapple.**

SERVES 4

Cut the fruit into pieces or leave them whole if small.
Layer in a large bowl, sprinkling each layer with sugar
and lemon juice. Allow to macerate for at least an hour.

VARIATION

Instead of lemon juice,
sprinkle with 4 tbsp cognac
or kirsch.

*1 KG/ 2 LB ORANGES,
CUT INTO 0.5 CM/ 1/4 IN SLICES*

*500G/ 1 LB/ 2 1/2 CUPS
GRANULATED SUGAR*

ORANGE SLICES IN SYRUP

**This preserve makes a ready sweet to serve with a
dollop of thick double (heavy) cream.**

SERVES 8–12

Put layers of orange slices and sugar in a pan. Cover
with water and cook gently for 1 1/2 hours, adding water to
keep the fruit covered.

When cool enough to handle, press the orange
slices into a jar and cover with syrup. Store in the
refrigerator (where they will keep well for weeks).

VARIATION

If you want the orange
slices to keep for several
months, use twice the
amount of sugar.

*1 KG/ 2 LB FRUIT – CHOOSE 2 OR
MORE FROM THE FOLLOWING:
APPLES, PEARS, PEACHES, PLUMS,
GREENGAGES, APRICOTS,
GOOSEBERRIES, CHERRIES AND
GRAPES*

450 ML/ 16 FL OZ/ 2 CUPS WATER

*100–250 G/ 4–9 OZ/ ½ –1¼
CUPS GRANULATED SUGAR*

VARIATIONS

As special flavouring, add
to the syrup the peel of a
lemon or an orange, the
juice of ½ lemon, a stick of
cinnamon, a few cloves or a
vanilla pod or a few drops
of vanilla essence (extract).

At the end, add a few
tablespoons of kirsch,
cognac or Cointreau.

Instead of water, you could
use a mixture of wine – red
or white – and water.

FRUIT COMPOTES

**Fresh fruits poached in sugar syrup make
an easy sweet. For a more glamorous
dessert they can be served on a bed of rice
pudding (see page 198) or on an almondy custard
cream (page 201).**

SERVES 4

Wash the fruit; peel, halve and stone it if necessary. Apples and pears should be peeled, cored and sliced.

To make the syrup, bring the water to the boil with the sugar. Start by using the lesser amount and add more during the cooking after tasting. The sweetness of the syrup is a matter of taste and the tartness of the particular fruit.

Put the fruit in the boiling syrup. Each fruit needs a different cooking time, which also depends on their degree of ripeness. Ripe fresh fruit should be poached very briefly. Cherries, gooseberries and grapes need only 1–3 minutes, apricots and plums require 5 minutes; peaches 10; apple slices 10–15 minutes; clementines with their peels (cut in half) may need 25 minutes; and pears, if they are unripe and hard, need more than 40 minutes. Orange slices and tangerines can be cooked for 1 hour. For mixed compotes it is best to poach the fruits separately or to add them at different times so that none is overcooked. Serve cold or chilled.

OVERLEAF *From left to right: Cherry,
Grape and Apricot Compotes*

700G/ 1 ½ LB/ 2 LARGE QUINCES

250G/ 9 OZ/ 1 ¼ CUPS
GRANULATED SUGAR

750ML/ 1 ¼ PINTS/ 3 ½ CUPS
WATER

150ML/ 5 FL OZ/ ⅔ CUP CLOTTED
OR THICK DOUBLE (HEAVY) CREAM

STEWED QUINCE

You will find this all over the Mediterranean, but in Turkey it is the most popular dessert. It is one of my favourites.

SERVES 4

Cut the quinces in half through the core. They are very hard and you need a strong knife and strong pressure to cut them. Trim the blackened ends, but leave the cores and seeds – they will provide a lovely characteristic jelly.

In a wide shallow pan, put the sugar and water (there should be enough to cover the quinces in one layer) and bring to the boil. Put in the fruit, cut side down, and simmer, covered, until it feels tender when you pierce it with the point of a knife. The cooking time can vary between 20 minutes to 1 hour depending on the quality and ripeness of the fruit.

Lift out the fruit and place it on a dish. When it is cool enough to handle, cut out the cores carefully. Boil down the syrup, uncovered, to a thick consistency (thick enough to coat the back of a spoon) – it turns a rich garnet red.

Return the fruit to the pan, cut side down, and cook in the syrup for 10 minutes.

Arrange in a serving dish, cut side up, with the syrup poured over. Serve with a dollop of cream in the centre, or pass the cream round so that people can help themselves.

1 LITRE/ 1 3/4 PINTS/ 4 1/2 CUPS WATER

250G/ 9 OZ/ 1 1/4 CUPS GRANULATED SUGAR

1/4 TSP GROUND GINGER

FEW DROPS VANILLA ESSENCE (EXTRACT)

4 LARGE YELLOW PEACHES

PEACHES IN A FRAGRANT SYRUP

These peaches are not too sweet; they have a very delicate vanilla and ginger flavour. There must be enough syrup to cover them and it can be re-used – to make another quantity if necessary. Use large yellow peaches that are firm and not too ripe.

SERVES 4

For the syrup, boil the water and sugar until the sugar is dissolved. Add the ginger and vanilla essence (extract) and remove from the heat.

To skin the peaches, drop them in boiling water (off the heat) and leave for a few minutes. Drain the peaches and slip off the skins. Poach the peeled peaches, whole, in the syrup for 15–20 minutes, until very tender. Leave them in the syrup until you are ready to eat. Serve chilled or at room temperature, without the syrup.

Serve with Almond Custard (see page 201) flavoured with a sweet wine such as Beaume de Vin de Pêches, with cassis or with Honey Icecream (see page 202).

8 PEACHES, CUT IN HALF,
UNPEELED, AND STONES REMOVED

120ML/ 3¹/₂ FL OZ/ ¹/₂ CUP
AMARETTO OR MARSALA

2–3 DROPS VANILLA ESSENCE

4 TBSP GRANULATED SUGAR,
OR TO TASTE

ROAST PEACHES

**This very simple and delicious way of
preparing peaches is from southern Italy.**

SERVES 4

Pre-heat the oven to 190°C/375°F/Gas 5.

Arrange the peaches in a shallow baking dish, cut side up. Mix the Amaretto or Marsala with the vanilla and 2 tbsp of the sugar, and pour over the peaches, so that a little settles in the hollows.

Bake for 10–20 minutes or until soft (the time varies, depending on the size and ripeness of the fruit).

Sprinkle the tops with the remaining sugar and put under the grill (broiler) until caramelized. The baking can be done in advance, but the last step must be carried out just before serving.

FOR THE RICE PUDDING

200G/7 OZ/1 CUP ROUND ITALIAN
OR PUDDING RICE

350ML/12 FL OZ/1¹/₂ CUPS WATER

1 LITRE/1³/₄ PINTS/4¹/₂ CUPS MILK

175G/6 OZ/³/₄ CUP GRANULATED
SUGAR, OR TO TASTE

2 TBSP ROSE WATER

¹/₂ TSP GROUND MASTIC

**FOR THE FRUITS
POACHED IN SYRUP**

250G/8 OZ/1 CUP GRANULATED
SUGAR

250ML/8 FL OZ/1 CUP WATER

JUICE OF ¹/₄ LEMON

3 PEACHES OR NECTARINES, PEELED
AND QUARTERED

3 PEARS, PEELED AND QUARTERED

6 APRICOTS, PITTED AND CUT
IN HALF

VARIATIONS

For an alternative
flavouring, add 1 tsp
ground cardamom at the
same time as the milk and
omit the mastic.

For alternative fruit
compotes, see page 191.

POACHED FRUIT ON
A RICE PUDDING BASE

**Mastic and rose water – two Arab flavourings –
give the rice pudding a delicious exotic
flavour that marries well with the stewed fruit
topping. Mastic is a resin from a tree which
you can buy in small 'grains' or crystals in Greek
and Middle Eastern stores. You have to pound
it yourself to a powder, with a little sugar, with a
pestle and mortar. You must use very little
as otherwise the taste is unpleasant. An
alternative to mastic is ground cardamom, which
is easy to come by and easier to use.**

SERVES 6

To make the rice pudding, put the rice in a large pan with the water. Bring to the boil and simmer for 8 minutes or until the water is absorbed. Add the milk and simmer over very low heat, stirring occasionally, for about 30–45 minutes until the rice is very soft and the milk is almost, but not entirely, absorbed. Add the sugar and stir until dissolved, then add the rose water and the mastic and stir vigorously. Pour into a wide shallow serving dish.

To make the fruit poached in syrup, put the sugar, water and lemon in a pan and bring to the boil, then simmer gently. Pour boiling water over the peaches or nectarines to loosen their skins, then peel them.

Put the different fruits in the syrup separately, in batches, because they cook at different rates. The time also depends on their size and degree of ripeness. Peaches and apricots can take 6 minutes only, and pears much longer. Turn the fruit pieces over once if they are not entirely covered by the syrup.

As they become tender, lift them out of the syrup onto a plate, to drain the excess syrup. Arrange them in a flower pattern on top of the rice pudding. Serve cold.

500G/1 LB BLACK CHERRIES

3 EGGS, SIZE 1 (U.S. LARGE)

100G/4 OZ/ 1/2 CUP CASTER (SUPERFINE) SUGAR

1 TBSP PLAIN (ALL-PURPOSE) FLOUR

2 DROPS VANILLA ESSENCE (EXTRACT)

2 TBSP CALVADOS OR KIRSCH

150ML/5 FL OZ/ 2/3 CUP DOUBLE (HEAVY) CREAM

100ML/4 FL OZ/ 1/2 CUP MILK

ICING (CONFECTIONERS') SUGAR TO SPRINKLE ON

CHERRY CLAFOUTIS

This old Provençal country dish of cherries baked in custard remains popular. There is no need to pit the cherries, but you can do so if you prefer.

SERVES 4

Pre-heat the oven to 180°C/350°F/Gas 4.

Wash and dry the cherries. Put them in a buttered shallow 22cm/8½in baking dish.

Beat the eggs with the sugar and flour. Add the vanilla and Calvados or kirsch, and gradually beat in the cream and milk.

Pour the mixture over the cherries and bake for about 45 minutes or until the cream sets and a light golden crust forms.

Serve warm, sprinkled with icing (confectioners') sugar. You may put it under the grill (broiler) for 1 minute until caramelized.

FOR THE SAUTÉED FRUIT

75G/ 3 OZ/ 6 TBSP UNSALTED BUTTER

3 APPLES, PEELED AND CUT INTO SMALL PIECES

2 PEARS, PEELED AND CUT INTO SMALL PIECES

6 APRICOTS, PITTED AND CUT INTO PIECES

A DOZEN OR MORE CHERRIES

3–4 TBSP GRANULATED SUGAR, OR TO TASTE

3 TBSP CALVADOS OR ARMAGNAC

FOR THE ALMOND CUSTARD

175G/ 6 OZ/ 3/4 CUP GRANULATED SUGAR

5 EGG YOLKS, SIZE 1 (U.S. LARGE)

75G/ 3 OZ/ 3/4 CUP PLAIN (ALL-PURPOSE) FLOUR

500ML/ 18 FL OZ/ 2 1/4 CUPS MILK

2–3 TBSP KIRSCH, RUM, CALVADOS OR ARMAGNAC

100G/ 4 OZ/ 1 CUP GROUND ALMONDS

3 DROPS ALMOND OR VANILLA ESSENCE (EXTRACT) (OPTIONAL)

SAUTÉED FRUIT WITH ALMOND CUSTARD

One of my favourite summer desserts is an assortment of fruit poached in syrup (see page 191) on an almond custard served chilled. In the winter, sautéed fruit on steaming hot custard is an irresistible sweet. All kinds of fruit can be sautéed. Grinding blanched almonds yourself in a food processor will give a better texture than using bought ground almonds. The almond essence is optional; in the past, the almond flavour was intensified by adding a few bitter almonds.

SERVES 6

To prepare the fruit, melt the butter in a large frying pan and sauté the apples and pears, stirring and turning them over occasionally, for 15 minutes, or until they are tender. Add the apricots and cherries and sauté briefly, until soft. Add the sugar and alcohol and cook for a few more minutes.

To make the custard, beat the sugar with the egg yolks to a light pale cream. Then beat in the flour.

Bring the milk to the boil in a heavy bottomed pan. Very gradually pour onto the egg mixture, beating vigorously until well blended, then pour the mixture back into the pan.

Simmer for 3 minutes longer, stirring constantly so that lumps do not form and the cream does not catch at the bottom. If the cream does slightly burn at the

VARIATIONS

Serve the almond custard cold topped with poached fruit (see pages 191 and 198).

Serve the cold almond custard as a bed for raw fruit, such as strawberries, raspberries, blueberries, white and black grapes, pitted fresh dates, sliced kiwi fruit and orange slices cut into small pieces.

500ML/ 18 FL OZ/ 2¼ CUPS MILK

4 EGG YOLKS, SIZE 1 (U.S. LARGE)

150G/ 5OZ LAVENDER, ACCACIA OR OTHER CLEAR, PERFUMED HONEY

150ML/ 5 FL OZ/ ⅔ CUP DOUBLE (HEAVY) CREAM

1 TBSP ORANGE BLOSSOM WATER

bottom, be careful not to scrape the burnt bits into the custard.

Stir in the alcohol, almonds and the almond or vanilla essence (extract) if using. Be careful to add only a few drops of almond essence, as too much is horrible. Cook for a few more moments.

Pour into a wide shallow serving dish and spoon the fruit with their juices all over the top.

If you want to prepare the custard in advance, pour the custard in a baking dish and heat it through in the oven. Pour the hot fruit on top just before serving.

HONEY ICECREAM

This fragrant icecream is a speciality of Provence where it is made with lavender honey.

SERVES 6

Boil the milk. Beat the egg yolks to a pale cream, then beat in the honey, the cream and, finally, the hot milk.

Return the mixture to the pan and stir with a wooden spoon over low heat until it thickens to a light cream, but do not let it boil or it will curdle. Then stir in the orange blossom water.

Let it cool and pour into a serving bowl. Cover with cling film (plastic wrap) and freeze overnight or at least 5 hours before serving. You may serve the icecream straight from the freezer.

250ML/ 8 FL OZ/ 1 CUP WATER

150–200G/ 5–7 OZ/ ¾ –1 CUP
GRANULATED SUGAR

JUICE OF 1 LEMON

1 KG/ 2 LB/ 5 PEARS, PEELED AND
CORED

POIRE WILLIAM LIQUEUR OR A
FRUIT BRANDY (OPTIONAL)

PEAR GRANITA

SERVES 4–6

In a wide pan that can hold the pears in one layer, boil the water and sugar with the lemon juice until the sugar melts. (Put in the lesser amount of sugar to start with and add more, if necessary, at the end, depending on the sweetness of the pears).

Put in the pears, and cook, covered, for 10 minutes or until they are soft.

Blend the pears with the syrup to a cream in a food processor. (Taste for sugar and add more if necessary.) Pour into ice cube trays, cover with cling film (plastic wrap), and leave the pulp to freeze hard overnight in the freezer.

Put the frozen cubes, in batches, in the food processor and process them into a very fine, frothy slush. Pour into a serving bowl and serve at once or return to the freezer, covered with cling film (plastic wrap).

Take out 10 minutes before you are ready to serve. If you like, pass around the pear liqueur or fruit brandy for people to help themselves to a drizzle.

250ML/ 8 FL OZ/ 1 CUP WATER

200G/ 7 OZ/ 1 CUP GRANULATED
SUGAR

JUICE OF 1/2 LEMON

1 KG/ 2 LB RIPE APRICOTS, PITTED

KIRSCH OR FRUIT BRANDY
(OPTIONAL)

APRICOT GRANITA

This water ice has a refreshingly tart flavour.

SERVES 4–6

Boil the water and sugar with the lemon juice in a wide pan until the sugar melts.

Put in the apricots and cook, covered, for 5 minutes or until they are very tender.

Blend the apricots with their syrup to a cream in a food processor. Pour into ice cube trays and cover with cling film (plastic wrap). Let the pulp freeze hard overnight in the freezer.

Put the frozen cubes, in batches, in the food processor and turn them into a very fine, frothy slush. Pour into a serving bowl and serve at once or return to the freezer, covered with cling film (plastic wrap).

Take out 10 minutes before you are ready to serve. If you like, pass around the kirsch or fruit brandy for people to help themselves to a tablespoon or so.

LEFT *Apricot Granita and Pear Granita (page 203)*

4 LARGE GOLDEN DELICIOUS APPLES, CORED AND SLICED

150ML/5 FL OZ/²/3 CUP FRUITY DRY WHITE WINE

100G/4 OZ/¹/2 CUP CASTER (SUPERFINE) SUGAR

3 EGG YOLKS, SIZE 1 (U.S. LARGE)

3 TBSP CALVADOS

150ML/5 FL OZ/²/3 CUP DOUBLE (HEAVY) CREAM

VARIATIONS

Add 3 drops vanilla essence (extract), a small stick of cinnamon and 2 cloves.

Pears may be used instead of apples with kirsch or Poire William.

FROZEN APPLE FOOL WITH CALVADOS

This is called a *parfait* in France.

SERVES 4

Put the apples and the white wine in a pan and simmer with the lid on for 5–10 minutes until the apples are soft. Remove the lid and cook on a higher heat to reduce the liquid.

Add half the sugar, mash the apples with a potato masher or fork, and cook, stirring, until the apple purée is thick and most of the liquid has disappeared.

Beat the egg yolks with the remaining sugar to a pale cream. Pour over the apple purée, off the heat, stirring vigorously, then stir over low heat for 30 seconds. Stir in the Calvados and chill in the refrigerator.

Whip the double (heavy) cream to firm peaks and fold into the cold apple purée. Pour into a bowl lined with cling film (plastic wrap) – this makes turning out easier. Cover the top with cling film (plastic wrap) and leave to freeze overnight.

Serve the fool straight from the freezer. Remove the covering cling film (plastic wrap), turn out on a serving plate, and remove the remaining cling film (plastic wrap).

4 EGG YOLKS, SIZE 1 (U.S. LARGE)

150G/5 OZ/³/₄ CUP CASTER
(SUPERFINE) SUGAR

300ML/10 FL OZ/1¹/₄ CUPS
SINGLE (LIGHT) CREAM

4 TBSP ARMAGNAC OR COGNAC

300ML/10 FL OZ/1¹/₄ CUPS
WHIPPING OR DOUBLE (HEAVY)
CREAM

200G/7 OZ MARRONS GLACÉS,
CUT INTO SMALL PIECES

SEMI-FREDDO
WITH MARRONS GLACÉS

**This is a splendid and luxurious sweet.
Italian food stores sell broken pieces of marrons
glacés, which work out very much cheaper
than the usual product.**

SERVES 4-6

Beat the yolks with the sugar to a pale light cream. Bring the single (light) cream to the boil, remove from the heat and beat it into the egg mixture.

Return the mixture to the pan and cook, stirring constantly over low heat, without letting it boil or it will curdle, until the cream is thick enough to coat the back of a spoon.

Add the Armagnac or cognac to the custard, let it cool, and put in the freezer for 1 hour, covered with cling film (plastic wrap).

Beat the whipping or double (heavy) cream until stiff and fold it into the cold custard, then fold in the marrons glacés.

To shape the icecream into a dome that is easy to unmould, line a bowl with cling film (plastic wrap) and pour the mixture in, cover with another piece of cling film (plastic wrap) and freeze overnight.

Remove the cling film (plastic wrap) and turn out just before serving.

200G/ 7 OZ CALIFORNIAN PITTED
PRUNES

85ML/ 3 FL·OZ/ 1/3 CUP ARMAGNAC
BRANDY

300ML/ 10 FL OZ/ 1 1/4 CUPS
WHIPPING CREAM

2 TBSP CASTER (SUPERFINE) SUGAR

2 DROPS VANILLA ESSENCE
(EXTRACT)

FROZEN CREAM WITH PRUNES AND ARMAGNAC

This light chantilly-type cream with a strong flavour of Armagnac is easy to make and tastes delicious.

SERVES 4

Chop the prunes coarsely in a food processor, add the Armagnac and soak for an hour.

Beat the whipping cream until it forms peaks, then beat in the sugar and vanilla essence (extract) and fold in the prunes and Armagnac.

Cover with cling film (plastic wrap) and freeze for at least 4 hours. You can serve the cream straight out of the freezer.

250G/9 OZ/1 1/4 CUPS MEDIUM COUSCOUS

ABOUT 300ML/10 FL OZ/1 1/4 CUPS WATER

6 TBSP GRANULATED SUGAR, OR TO TASTE

2 TBSP GROUNDNUT (PEANUT) OR SUNFLOWER OIL

125G/4 1/2 OZ/3/4 CUP MIXED NUTS, SUCH AS WALNUTS, BLANCHED ALMONDS, HAZELNUTS, PISTACHIOS AND PINE NUTS

1/2 X 225G/8 OZ BOX CALIFORNIA DATES, PITTED AND CUT INTO PIECES

300ML/10 FL OZ/1 1/4 CUPS HOT MILK

SWEET COUSCOUS WITH NUTS AND DATES

Couscous is the Berber food of North Africa. This sweet couscous is more of a breakfast dish or afternoon snack than an after-dinner dessert. It is tasty and satisfying comfort food.

SERVES 4

Pre-heat the oven to 200°C/400°F/Gas 6.

Put the couscous in a round ovenproof serving dish. Boil the water with 4 tbsp of the sugar and all of the oil. Pour over the couscous and stir well. Leave for about 15 minutes, stirring occasionally, until the water has been absorbed.

Rub the grain between your hands to remove any lumps that stick together. Add more sugar if it is not sweet enough to your taste.

Toast the nuts very lightly under the grill (broiler) or in a dry pan and chop them coarsely. Stir them into the grain with the dates. Cover the dish with a lid or with foil and heat through for 20 minutes in the oven. This will have a steaming effect.

Heat the milk and serve the couscous hot, accompanied by the milk and extra sugar for people to pour over it.

NOTE You may heat the couscous in a saucepan with a lid instead of in the oven, but you will need to stir it often so that it does not burn at the bottom.

100G/ 4 OZ/ ½ CUP
SOFTENED UNSALTED BUTTER

3 EGGS, SIZE 1 (U.S. LARGE)

150G/ 5 OZ/ ¾ CUP CASTER
(SUPERFINE) SUGAR

150G/ 5 OZ/ 1 ¼ CUPS COARSELY
GROUND BLANCHED ALMONDS

2–3 DROPS ALMOND ESSENCE
(EXTRACT)

1 KG/ 2 LB. APRICOTS, PITTED AND
CUT IN HALF

2 TBSP ICING (CONFECTIONERS')
SUGAR

POT OF DOUBLE (HEAVY) CREAM,
TO SERVE

FOR THE SAUCE

200G/ 7 OZ/ 1 CUP SMOOTH OR
'JELLY' APRICOT JAM

3 TBSP WATER

1–2 TBSP KIRSCH OR APRICOT
BRANDY

VARIATION

Use pears, peeled, cored,
cut in half and boiled for
about 15 minutes or until
almost tender, instead of
apricots.

APRICOT AND ALMOND PUDDING

**Apricots give this old Provençal speciality
a refreshing tartness.**

SERVES 6

Pre-heat the oven to 180°C/350°F/Gas 4.

Blend the butter and eggs with the sugar in a food processor. Add the almonds and almond essence (extract) and continue to blend to a soft cream. Pour into a 30cm/12in baking dish.

Arrange the apricot halves on top, cut side down, pressing them into the paste. Bake for about 45 minutes or until the paste is firm and lightly coloured.

To make the sauce, heat the apricot jam with the water and kirsch or apricot brandy and stir until it melts. Let the sauce cool.

Serve the pudding cold, sprinkled with icing (confectioners') sugar. Accompany with the sauce and a bowl of cream.

500G/ 1 LB RICOTTA

150G/ 5 OZ/ ³/₄ CUP CASTER
(SUPERFINE) SUGAR, OR TO TASTE

5 EGGS, SIZE 1 (U.S. LARGE),
SEPARATED

2 TSP ORANGE BLOSSOM WATER

GRATED ZEST OF ¹/₂ LEMON

75G/ 3 OZ/ ¹/₃ CUP DICED CANDIED
ORANGE PEEL

VARIATION

Use a few drops of vanilla
essence (extract) or 1½ tsp
cinnamon instead of orange
blossom water.

RICOTTA CAKE

**This rich Sicilian cake is a bit like a soufflé.
The orange blossom water is a legacy of the old
Arab occupation of the island.**

SERVES 8

Pre-heat the oven to 180°C/350°F/Gas 4.

In a food processor, blend the ricotta, sugar, egg
yolks, orange blossom water and grated lemon zest to a
homogenous cream.

Fold in the diced candied orange peel.

Beat the egg whites until stiff, then fold into the
ricotta mixture.

Pour into a greased and floured, preferably non-
stick 20cm/8in cake tin and bake for 45 minutes or until
brown on top. The cake rises quite high. Let it cool
before turning out.

100G/4 OZ DARK BITTER CHOCOLATE

50G/2 OZ/4 TBSP UNSALTED BUTTER

4 EGGS, SIZE 1 (U.S. LARGE), SEPARATED

100G/4 OZ/1/2 CUP CASTER (SUPERFINE) SUGAR

CHOCOLATE CAKE

This has such a wonderful creamy-soft texture that it is more of a pudding than a cake.

SERVES 6

Pre-heat the oven to 150°C/300°F/Gas 2.

Melt the chocolate and butter in a heatproof bowl over a pan of boiling water.

Beat the egg yolks and the sugar to a pale light cream, then beat in the chocolate mixture.

Beat the egg whites until stiff and fold them into the chocolate and egg mixture.

Pour into a buttered, preferably non-stick 20cm/8in cake tin and bake for 30 minutes. Leave it in the oven for 30 minutes before turning out (it comes out easily). Let it cool before serving.

500G/1 LB/4¹/2 CUPS GROUND ALMONDS

200G/7 OZ/1 CUP CASTER (SUPERFINE) SUGAR

1¹/2 TSP CINNAMON

3 DROPS (NO MORE) ALMOND ESSENCE (EXTRACT) (OPTIONAL)

2 TBSP ORANGE BLOSSOM WATER

4 EGG YOLKS, SIZE 1 (U.S. LARGE)

5 SHEETS OF FILO PASTRY

3–4 TBSP UNSALTED BUTTER, MELTED, OR SUNFLOWER OIL

ICING (CONFECTIONERS') SUGAR, FOR DUSTING

MOROCCAN ALMOND 'SNAKE'

This is a good pastry to make for a party. It is very rich, so serve it in small pieces. It takes its Moroccan name *m'hencha* from the word *hencha*, meaning snake, because it looks like a curled snake.

SERVES 12 OR MORE

Pre-heat the oven to 180°C/350°F/Gas 4.

In a bowl, mix the ground almonds, sugar, ¹/2 tsp of the cinnamon and the almond essence (extract) if using. Add the orange blossom water and 3 egg yolks, and combine well with your hands.

Open the packet of filo only when you are ready to use the pastry. Take 5 sheets out and keep them in a pile. Brush the top one lightly with melted butter.

Press the almond paste with your hand into long thin sausages the thickness of a thumb, and place them end to end, making a rod of paste along one long edge of the filo sheet, about 2 cm/¾ in from the end.

Lift the pastry edge up over the paste and roll up into a loose, long thin roll. To curve this roll without tearing the pastry, wrinkle the pastry first by pressing the ends of the roll gently towards the middle.

Lift the pastry roll carefully onto the middle of a greased flat ovenproof dish or a sheet of foil on a baking tray, and curve it gently into a snail shape.

Continue in the same way with the rest of the filling and sheets of filo, placing the long, wrinkled rolls end to end, curving them to make a long coil.

Brush the top with the remaining egg yolk mixed with a teaspoon of water, and bake for 45 minutes until crisp and browned on top.

Serve cold, dusted with icing (confectioners') sugar and a sprinkling of the remaining cinnamon.

BASICS

PREPARATIONS

TO CLEAN AND PREPARE SQUID

Pull the head away from the body pouch and discard the soft innards that come out with it. Discard the insides of the pouch – the inkbag, if any, the icicle-shaped transparent cuttlebone and the soft innards. Keep the tentacles in their bunches but remove the eyes and the small round cartilage at the base of the tentacles by cutting with a sharp knife just above the eyes (be careful that ink doesn't squirt out at you from the eyes). Rinse thoroughly. Cut the body into rings.

TO CLEAN AND PREPARE MUSSELS

Scrub the mussels, pull off the beards and wash in several changes of cold water. Test to see if they are alive: discard any that are broken and those that are too heavy or too light, or do not close when they are tapped or dipped in cold water. To steam them open, put them in a large pan with a finger of water and the lid on. Take off the heat as soon as they open (in about 1 minute). Discard any that remain closed.

TO ROAST AND PEEL (BELL) PEPPERS

Many dishes call for roasted (bell) peppers. Choose fleshy peppers. Put them on an oven tray under the grill (broiler), about 9cm/3½in from the grill (broiler) (or grill them on the barbecue). Turn them until their skins are black and blistered all over.

Alternatively, it is easier to roast them in a 180°C/350°F/Gas 4 oven for 1 hour (or the hottest oven for 30 minutes) until they are soft and their skins begin to blister and blacken. They need to be turned once during the roasting. To loosen the skins further, put them in a pan with a tight-fitting lid or in a strong polythene (polyethylene) bag and twist it closed. Leave for 10–15 minutes. This helps to loosen the skins. When the peppers are cool enough to handle, peel them and remove the stems and seeds. Reserve the juice that comes out and strain to remove the seeds as the juice can be used as part of the dressing.

Roast peppers can be kept, covered with oil, for several months. Store them in a cool, dark place.

To Grill (Broil) or Roast Aubergine (Eggplant) Slices

These days many people prefer grilled (broiled) or roasted aubergines (eggplants) to fried ones, but very often they are not cooked enough.

Cut the aubergines (eggplants) into 0.5–1cm/ ¼–⅓in slices, lengthways or into rounds, sprinkle with salt and let them degorge their juices for half an hour. Rinse and dry them. (This process can be omitted if the aubergines (eggplants) are not particularly bitter – it is not always necessary.) Brush both sides generously with oil and turn under the grill (broiler) or over a charcoal fire.

Alternatively, lay them on an oven tray and bake in a very hot oven until tender and lightly browned.

To Prepare Hearts of Small Globe Artichokes

With a small sharp knife, cut off the stalk and cut away or pull off the tough outer leaves, starting at the base, until you are left with the pale inner leaves. Then slice off the tough ends of these, open them out and scoop out the prickly inner choke with a pointed spoon.

To Prepare Bottoms of Large Globe Artichokes

Cut away all the leaves to the bare flat bottom with a sharp pointed knife, then cut or scrape away the chokes from the centre.

RECIPES

VINAIGRETTE

**In the Mediterranean lemon juice is often used
in a salad dressing instead of vinegar.**

SALT AND PEPPER

*1 TBSP WHITE OR RED WINE
VINEGAR OR LEMON JUICE*

*3½ TBSP LIGHT EXTRA VIRGIN
OLIVE OIL*

Stir the salt and pepper into the vinegar until the salt
is dissolved. Then beat in the oil.

FRESH TOMATO SAUCE

**This sauce can be used for many dishes
including sautéed fish and pasta.**

MAKES ENOUGH TO SERVE 4–6

*1–2 GARLIC CLOVES, FINELY
CHOPPED OR CRUSHED*

2–3 TBSP EXTRA VIRGIN OLIVE OIL

*8 RIPE PLUM TOMATOES, PEELED
AND CHOPPED*

SALT AND PEPPER

1–2 TSP GRANULATED SUGAR

Sauté the garlic lightly in the oil over low heat until the
aroma rises. Add the tomatoes, salt, pepper and sugar
and simmer for 10–15 minutes to reduce slightly.

VARIATIONS

Add 3 tbsp chopped parsley or basil.

Add 1 tbsp fresh grated ginger or the juice of a 2.5cm/1in
piece of ginger, peeled and crushed in a garlic press.

A Moroccan version uses ½ tsp ground ginger, ¼ tsp saffron
and ¼ tsp chilli pepper. It is sometimes garnished with 6 or
7 olives and ½ chopped preserved lemon peel (see page 219).

PRESERVED LEMON PEELS

This preserve, often used chopped up as a garnish, gives an unusual mellow lemony flavour to many North African dishes, from salads to seafood.

Wash the lemons and make two vertical cuts in a cross, almost but not quite through the lemons, so that the sections still hold together at the stem. Sprinkle about 125g/4oz/½ cup salt for 1kg/2lb (about 8) lemons inside on the cut flesh, then close them and pack them tightly in a clean jar. Squeeze enough fresh lemon juice over them to cover. The salt will draw out the juices and the peel will soften within a week. Cover and store in a cool dark place. They will be ready to use in 3–4 weeks.

Rinse off the salt before using and discard the flesh. It is the peel alone that you want.

50G/2 OZ DRIED HOT RED CHILLI PEPPERS (STEMS AND SEEDS REMOVED)

4 GARLIC CLOVES, PEELED

1 TSP GROUND CARAWAY

1 TSP GROUND CORIANDER

ABOUT ½ TSP SALT

EXTRA VIRGIN OLIVE OIL

HARISSA

This hot chilli paste is used in many North African dishes.

MAKES ABOUT 225ML/8FL OZ/1 CUP

Soak the chilli peppers in water for 30 minutes until soft. Drain and pound with the garlic, spices and a little salt with a pestle and mortar, or blend in a food processor, adding just enough oil, by the tablespoon, to make a soft paste. Press the mixture into a jar and cover with oil. This way it keeps very well, for several weeks, in the refrigerator.

1 EGG YOLK, SIZE 1 (U.S. LARGE)

JUICE OF ¹/₂–1 LEMON

¹/₂ TSP SALT

*300ML/10 FL OZ/1¹/₄ CUPS OIL –
A MIXTURE OF SUNFLOWER OR
LIGHT VEGETABLE OIL WITH EXTRA
VIRGIN OLIVE OIL*

*4 GARLIC CLOVES OR MORE, TO
TASTE, CRUSHED IN A PRESS OR
POUNDED TO A PASTE (IF YOU ARE
MAKING AIOLI)*

MAYONNAISE AND AIOLI

Aïoli is the garlic mayonnaise common to
Spain and southern France. It is made in the same
way as mayonnaise but with added garlic.
It is used as a dip for crudités, and with boiled
vegetables or fish and seafood.
It is best not to use olive oil alone as the
result is too strong and overpowering. Instead,
use a mixture of a bland vegetable oil and
olive oil. The proportions may vary. I like to use
²/₃ vegetable oil and ¹/₃ olive oil. It is usual
to beat the garlic with the egg yolk first until pale
and creamy but you may prefer to add it at
the end when you can taste and decide how much
you want to put in.
To ensure success, all the ingredients must be at
room temperature (do not use an egg straight from
the refrigerator) and the bowl should be warm.

MAKES 400ML/14FL OZ/1³/₄ CUPS

VARIATION

For a rouille, which goes
very well with fish soup,
add 1–2 tsp paprika and a
good pinch of cayenne.

Put the egg yolk in a warmed bowl (place it on a wet
cloth to prevent it from slipping). Add some of the lemon
juice and a little salt.

Add the oil, a little at a time – first drop by drop,
then in a thin stream – beating vigorously all the time
with an electric whisk.

As the oil becomes absorbed the sauce will thicken
to a heavy, thick consistency.

Finally, beat in the garlic and the rest of the lemon
juice, to taste.

1 TBSP ACTIVE DRY YEAST

PINCH OF GRANULATED SUGAR

*ABOUT (A LITTLE LESS THAN)
450ML/ 16 FL OZ/ 2 CUPS
LUKEWARM WATER*

*750G/ 1 LB 10 OZ/ 5¼ CUPS
STRONG (UNBLEACHED HARD-
WHEAT) WHITE FLOUR*

2 TSP SALT

*5 TBSP EXTRA VIRGIN OLIVE OIL
(PLUS A LITTLE TO GREASE THE
DOUGH AND PAN)*

FOCACCIA

**Flatbreads are very common throughout the
Mediterranean region. They are usually quite soft,
often flavoured with herbs or spices and
sometimes embellished with ingredients such as
chopped olives, fried onions and tomato pulp. In the
Arab world they can be sprinkled with sesame, fennel,
caraway, anis or onion seed, or with mixtures of
thyme, sesame and ground sumac. My favourite for
making at home is the versatile Italian focaccia,
made with olive oil, which has become immensely
popular in Britain and the United States. This recipe
is for basic focaccia. Several variations follow.**

SERVES 6–8

Dissolve the yeast and sugar in about half the measured
warm water. Leave for 10 minutes until it froths.

Put the flour and salt in a large bowl, and make a
well in the centre. Pour in the yeast mixture and 3 tbsp
of the oil and mix with a wooden spoon.

Add the remaining warm water very gradually –
just enough to make a soft ball that holds together,
mixing first with the wooden spoon, then working it in
with your hand.

Turn onto a lightly floured surface and knead for
about 10 minutes until very smooth and elastic, adding a
little flour if too sticky, or a drop of water if too dry.

Pour a little oil in the bowl and turn the dough in it
to grease it all over. Cover the bowl with cling film (plastic
wrap) and leave to rise in a warm place for about 1½ hours
or until doubled in bulk.

Punch the dough down and knead very briefly to punch out the air, then flatten all over the bottom of 1 or 2 oiled baking pans or sheets, pressing it down with oiled hands. I use 2 round 28cm/11in pans, but a large rectangular one will do very well. As the dough is very elastic and springs back, you may need to stretch it again a few times. A focaccia can be thick or thin, and the flattened dough can be from 0.5–1.25cm/about ¼–½in thick. Cover with a towel or foil and leave to rise again in a warm place for about 45 minutes. Pre-heat the oven to 220°C/425°F/Gas 7 for at least 30 minutes before baking. If you have a baking stone put it in.

Just before baking, make many deep holes all over the dough with your finger, and sprinkle or brush all over with the remaining olive oil.

Place the focaccia pans (one at a time) in the pre-heated oven. Bake for 30 minutes or until the crusts are crisp and golden. Turn out and place on a rack. Focaccia can be served at room temperature but is best eaten hot or warm. You may also freeze it. To serve, cut into squares, rectangles or wedges.

VARIATIONS

Before baking:

Sprinkle 1½ teaspoons coarse sea salt over the top.

Sprinkle with 2–3 chopped garlic cloves and the needles of 2 sprigs of rosemary or 2 tablespoons chopped sage leaves.

Sprinkle with 1 tablespoon chopped oregano and 75g/3oz black olives, pitted and finely chopped.

Spread with Tomato Sauce (see page 218), reduced until the liquid has disappeared, and sprinkle with 1 tablespoon chopped oregano, 3 chopped garlic cloves, and 8 pitted, halved black olives.

Brush with 3 tablespoons anchovy paste or 3 tablespoons olive paste mixed with 2 tablespoons olive oil.

Top with 2 large onions, sliced and fried in 3 tablespoons extra virgin oil over very low heat for about 45 minutes until very soft, covering the pan to begin with, and stirring occasionally. You can let the onions brown and caramelize, if you wish.

Roast and peel 3 red peppers (see page 216), cut them into ribbons and scatter over the dough with 3 chopped garlic cloves.

INDEX

Page numbers in *italics* refer
to illustrations